The
Multiple Menu Model

A Practical Guide for Developing
Differentiated Curriculum

Joseph S. Renzulli
Jann H. Leppien
Thomas S. Hays

Editor
Rachel Knox

Creative Learning Press, Inc.
P. O. Box 320, Mansfield Center, CT 06250
888-518-8004 • www.creativelearningpress.com

Do You Know Your Ologies and Ographies?

Match each -ology or -ography with its definition.

1.	Aerology	a.	evil spirits
2.	Anthropology	b.	the earth's changing surface
3.	Araenology	c.	aging
4.	Archaeology	d.	descriptions of specific cultures
5.	Astronomy	e.	motion picture photography
6.	Audiology	f.	contagious diseases
7.	Cardiology	g.	weather and climate
8.	Cartography	h.	handwriting
9.	Cetology	i.	word origins
10.	Choreography	j.	birds
11.	Chronology	k.	time sequence
12.	Cinematography	l.	dance
13.	Cryptology	m.	population, size, density, and distribution
14.	Crystallography	n.	existence, being
15.	Cytology	o.	whales
16.	Demography	p.	producing images with light.
17.	Demonology	q.	living tissue
18.	Dermatology	r.	rocks
19.	Ecology	s.	the sense of hearing
20.	Entomology	t.	bones
21.	Epidemiology	u.	the ear
22.	Epistemology	v.	the skin
23.	Ethnography	w.	knowledge
24.	Etymology	x.	the atmosphere in relation to flying
25.	Gemology	y.	the past through its materials and remains
26.	Genealogy	z.	ancient writing
27.	Geography	aa.	classification of crystals
28.	Geology	bb.	fossils
29.	Gerontology	cc.	fish
30.	Graphology	dd.	the earth's crust
31.	Herpetology	ee.	deciphering codes
32.	Histology	ff.	printing from a plane surface
33.	Holography	gg.	spiders
34.	Hydrology	hh.	gems
35.	Ichthyology	ii.	insects
36.	Laryngology	jj.	ancestry
37.	Lithography	kk.	prison and punishment
38.	Meteorology	ll.	cells
39.	Myrmecology	mm.	laser light to produce images
40.	Oceanography	nn.	ants
41.	Ontology	oo.	human races
42.	Ornithology	pp.	the stars
43.	Osteology	qq.	organisms and their environments
44.	Otology	rr.	reptiles
45.	Paleography	ss.	the mind, emotions, and behavior.
46.	Paleontology	tt.	ocean environments
47.	Penology	uu.	the heart
48.	Petrology	vv.	the throat
49.	Photography	ww.	water
50.	Psychology	xx.	mapping

Answers in Figure 5.2 on page 75.

To our friend and mentor,
Virgil Scott Ward,
whose wisdom and insights
are reflected in many ways
throughout this book
and whose contributions
to the larger world of knowledge
have inspired the creative productivity
of numerous people around the world.

Contents

Figures

Acknowledgments

No work is a solitary act. A number of individuals contributed to the development of *The Multiple Menu Model: A Practical Guide for Developing Differentiated Curriculum*. We would like to give a special thanks to the teachers enrolled in the Three Summers Master's Program at the University of Connecticut. They field tested and used chapters of the book as it was being written and contributed suggestions and ideas which we incorporated into the book. We are grateful for their dedication to their students, and we have been inspired as they have used the Multiple Menu Model to write curriculum. We have tried to honor them by placing examples of their curricular ideas within the text. We would like to give a special thanks to Gail Pattison for allowing us to present her unit on archaeology as an example of how teachers can use the Multiple Menu Model.

We also appreciate the countless conversations that we held with our colleagues who taught or used the Multiple Menu Model in its beginning phases: Sally Reis, Karen Westberg, E. Jean Gubbins, Marcia Imbeau, Deborah Burns, Sally Dobyns, and Jeanne Purcell. They shared their ideas regarding curriculum design and what it means to instruct students in meaningful ways. In addition, we would like to thank Karen Kettle who offered suggestions and reviewed early editions of the manuscript.

We would also like to acknowledge Rachel Knox who spent many hours on the editing and layout of this publication. Likewise, we thank, Lari Hatley, writer, friend, and educator, and Susanna Richards for their editorial assistance.

Finally, we want to thank our families who encouraged us in this effort by allowing us to spend numerous hours writing this book.

Foreword

It was just a journal article a mere twelve pages long. But when I first read "The Multiple Menu Model for Developing Differentiated Curriculum for the Gifted and Talented" by Joe Renzulli in 1988, missing pieces from my teaching life clicked into places where they belonged. Terms new to me gave clarity to fuzzier instincts that had fueled my own curriculum design. Most significantly, my sense of possibility was sent soaring. It's hard to be passionate about most journal articles, but this one was a thing of elegant conceptualization and practical possibility.

It was just a journal article, but as a classroom teacher, the Multiple Menu Model helped me in a myriad of ways. It showed me a seldom made link between curriculum theory and the craft of curriculum writing. It bonded curricular content and instructional decisions—a murky alignment in much of my own educational past. It helped me see how the actual practice of a discipline stems from the inherent nature of that discipline. More importantly, it made clear how, as a curriculum developer, my work must be shaped by how experts in a field organize their thinking, do their work, and assess the quality of their outcomes. The article affirmed my experience that a teacher's own joy in ideas ignites a curiosity in young learners.

It was just a journal article, but it followed me from my own public school classroom to my university teaching opportunity, and, over the past decade, it has been central in the work that my graduate students and I have done with curriculum at the University of Virginia. Because it was just a journal article, only allowed to take up a certain amount of space between other articles, the piece left unanswered questions about the author's terminology, thinking, and intent. Frequently over the past ten years, my students and I turned to Joe Renzulli for clarification and elaboration, but when we could not corner him by phone or at a conference for a fuller explanation of this point or that, my students and I crafted our own answers to the questions.

Now the Multiple Menu Model is no longer contained in just a journal article. It is elaborated, illustrated, and clarified. I am once again excited as I read.

This guide—as was the case with the article that preceded it—accomplishes several highly worthwhile goals. It provides one of the most useful contemporary frameworks that I know of for curricular and instructional design. While the model's ideas are practical, clear, and illustrated, it still reminds me that curriculum development is a high art. To make it less compromises both the lives of learners and the knowledge that could enhance those lives. The model provides structure to scaffold my thinking, but limits my freedom only as much as it demands that I surround my students with learning opportunities that are authentic and coherent.

For a decade now, I have watched my graduate students labor with the Knowledge Menu—trying to see the disciplines as expert practitioners know them rather than as textbook writers predigest them. I have watched these educators strive to align key concepts and principles with curriculum as they have known it or as it is mandated for them to teach. I have seen them wrestle with developing significant student products that invite learners to see ideas and skills as replete with possibilities in a real world. I have looked on as they seek to develop instructional sequences and approaches that balance a student's need to discover ideas with the teacher's need to ensure competence and clarity of understanding.

In all of that, I have watched these educators experience what we would want for the learners in their classrooms. At the end of an honest struggle, knowledge, understanding, and skill are living things. At the end of genuine challenge, the learner is remade.

I am so pleased to be a beneficiary of the work of all those whose efforts have amplified the journal article, those who have applied its precepts and shared the application with us in the form of this book. I look forward to using this resource to apply and extend my sense of what it means to be an architect of worthy curriculum and instruction. I am excited that my students will have this framework to help them refine their sense of how teachers discover authentic knowledge and use it to link students to the limitless possibilities of becoming a learning apprentice in a doing-to-know environment.

Carol Ann Tomlinson
The University of Virginia
August, 2000

Introduction:
A Sense of Things to Come

   This book emerged from our work over the last ten years in looking for strategies teachers can use to improve the curriculum writing process. Overloaded with volumes of state curriculum guides, caught on a seesaw between the importance of authentic knowledge (content) and instructional techniques (process), and challenged to include activities from the latest educational bandwagon, the Herculean task of curriculum writing often falls to an intrepid committee relegated to work during summer vacation. Their stories of frustration are common, and the ever present black, three-ring curriculum binder that sits on their colleagues' shelves collecting dust serves as a reminder that their work is not always relevant to their colleagues' instructional needs. While the curriculum writers' intentions are good and the work is rigorous, we have all come to realize that the hours of toil often result in a conglomeration of activities that does little to enhance the teaching and learning process in any meaningful way.

   It is our belief that in order for a curriculum guide to be effectively applied to the learning process in the regular classroom, teachers must be equipped with the tools and the time to translate these lists of curricular outcomes into meaningful units of instruction. The Multiple Menu Model respects this goal by providing six practical planning guides or menus that all teachers, K-12, can use to design in-depth curriculum units for classroom use. It is based on the work of theorists in curriculum and instruction (Ausubel, 1968; Bandura, 1977; Bloom, 1954; Bruner 1960, 1966; Gagné & Briggs, 1979; Kaplan, 1986; Passow, 1982; Phenix, 1964; and Ward, 1961) and differs from traditional approaches to curriculum design in that it places a greater emphasis on balancing authentic content and process, involving students as firsthand inquirers, and exploring the structure and interconnectedness of knowledge.

   We chose to create a "menu" because, like the choices that appear in the pull down menus of many computer software programs or on a restaurant menu, it provides the teacher-as-curriculum-designer with a range of options within each of the components of the model. The menus encourage teachers to design in-depth curriculum units that bring together an understanding of the structure of a discipline, its content and methodologies, and the wide range of instructional techniques educators use to create teaching and learning experiences.

Several assumptions and beliefs about curriculum development are inherent in the Multiple Menu Model. These assumptions provide the foundation for this model and help clarify the role of the teacher, the learner, and the curriculum. First and foremost, we believe that teachers who are able to inspire young people to explore a discipline have a genuine interest or passion in the discipline themselves. These teachers have gathered stories, realia, and documents to make the curriculum authentic, and they employ strategies to effectively engage learners in the process of inquiry. Second, we believe authentic learning consists of investigative activities and the development of creative products in which students assume roles as firsthand explorers, writers, artists, and other types of practicing professionals. Therefore, the overriding purpose of curriculum development should be to create situations in which young people are thinking, feeling, and doing what practicing professionals do when they explore the content and methodology of a particular discipline.

The Multiple Menu Model is designed for individual or small groups of teachers who want to write comprehensive curricula and who understand that this endeavor is rewarding but time consuming. The chapters in this how-to book offer more suggestions and guidelines than any one teacher could possibly use. As a teacher, you will need to be selective in your choices. Along the way, the chapters address issues, questions, and quandaries with which we, and the teachers with whom we work, have struggled. Several vignettes appear throughout the book to illustrate how teachers have used the Multiple Menu Model.

1

Blending Content with Instructional Technique

*Thinking ability is not a substitute for knowledge;
nor is knowledge a substitute for thinking ability.
Both are essential. Knowledge and thinking
are two sides of the same coin.*

—*R. S. Nickerson*

Anyone who sets out to develop curriculum will come face to face with two unavoidable realizations. First, developing curriculum is a difficult and demanding process. It involves far more thought and work than "slapping together" some content and a few process development activities, no matter how exciting these activities may be. An extraordinary amount of effort is necessary to produce material that reflects the established curricular principles and creates authentic, relevant, and personally meaningful instructional activities.

A second realization is that present day curriculum writers generally agree about underlying principles for developing curriculum. Most of these principles, invariably phrased as "should statements," point out the need for curricular experiences that focus on identifying the curriculum standards to be addressed in the unit of instruction, focusing instruction on abstract concepts, selecting the content and process skills that will be introduced to the students and used to develop student activities, and determining the assessment devices to judge student performance and acquisition of knowledge. These same "should" lists typically include principles that call for cooperative efforts between content scholars and teachers or instructional specialists in designing the curriculum. However, these principles are far too general to provide the kinds of specific guidance necessary for the practical job of writing curricular units of instruction. Knowing, for example, that a curricular unit should focus on higher level thinking skills and advanced content is valuable, but this knowledge does not tell curriculum writers how to identify appropriate content or skills, how to examine various instructional sequence and activity options, or how to prepare a blueprint for fitting together the pieces that will allow content and process to work together in a harmonious and effective fashion.

The Need for a Curriculum Model or Framework

Curriculum developers are, by definition, pragmatists—they must come up with tangible, practical outcomes. At the same time, they need guidance in overcoming the practical problems that are typically encountered in curriculum development. To do their work, curriculum developers need both the principles of the idealist and the practical models that will allow them to translate principles into concrete products. The best way to illustrate the need for practical models is to consider the typical problems presented in the following two scenarios:

Scenario I: The Content Expert

Dr. Cecil is a well known professor of mythology who has published several books and articles in his field. His classes are very popular, informative, entertaining, and highly rated by students. His method of instruction is based on a traditional and almost universal pattern in higher education. He presents lectures and assigns textbook chapters and related readings, and although discussions are not a formal part of his "lesson plan," they sometimes take place as a result of student questions. Students generally take copious notes, and they complete a term paper on an assigned topic. Dr. Cecil uses the paper plus an examination to evaluate student achievement. When asked about the objectives for his mythology course, Dr. Cecil paused for a moment, asked for a clarification of the question, and then replied, "I want my students to have a better knowledge and understanding of mythology."

Scenario II: The Instructional Expert

Ms. Bollin is an extremely popular and a well-respected middle school English teacher who teaches a unit on mythology each year. The class reads and discusses several myths, and students participate in mythological simulations and artistic and dramatic portrayals of myths. She encourages students to create their own mythological characters (both visually and in written form) and invites those students who show an interest in and talent for this topic to write original myths. Although she uses a wide variety of instructional techniques, Ms. Bollin fails to cover most of the essential concepts that define the field of mythology. When asked about her objectives for teaching the unit, she responded immediately by saying, "I want my students to be able to analyze, synthesize, and evaluate myths." She paused for a moment and then added, "I also want them to develop their creative thinking skills, self-concept, and interpersonal relations."

These two scenarios point out one of the enduring problems that educators face when considering the complexity of developing curriculum: balancing rigor and authenticity with instructional techniques that accommodate individual differences. No one would question the credentials of the college professor. He can obviously provide his students with an authentic knowledge base for the study of mythology. At the same time, there are few educators who would argue against the assertion that the "college teaching model" allows for few variations in the instructional process to accommodate individual differences in student abilities or interests. The attributes of subject matter rigor and authenticity are commendable, but the instructional techniques might cause classroom teachers who strive to meet diverse needs to raise questions about the lack of variety in the presentation of the curricular material.

The second scenario describes instructional techniques that are certainly more commensurate with the principles of good instruction. Yet, one cannot ignore the plain fact that knowledge about the subject matter is being dealt with in a less than authentic manner. The teacher described in the second scenario is as masterful in the use of instructional technique as the professor is in his command of the knowledge base. What is clearly needed is some kind of synthesis of the subject matter expert and the instructional expert. Bridging the gap between the knowledge of the content expert and knowledge of the instructional expert in a manner that assists curriculum writers is paramount if teachers are to design curriculum that is authentic, relevant, and personally meaningful to the students.

2

Understanding the Rationale of the Multiple Menu Model

To be interested in, wrapped up in, carried away by, some object.
To take an interest is to be on the alert, to care about, to be
attentive. We say of an interested person
that he has both lost himself in some affair and
that he has found himself in it. Both terms express the
engrossment of self in subject.

—*John Dewey*

In order to design effective curriculum, the curriculum writer must first understand how knowledge within a discipline is constructed. Disciplines have evolved as discrete entities over centuries as the result of the different kinds of questions researchers have asked and the different research methodologies they have developed to answer them. We have created the Multiple Menu Model to help curriculum designers use the information on how knowledge develops to create interesting and more authentic units of instruction. When the designer understands how knowledge develops, choices about which content and which instructional approaches to use in the unit become explicit.

A Brief Theory of Knowledge

The theory of knowledge underlying the Multiple Menu Model is based on the three levels of knowing first suggested by the American psychologist and philosopher, William James (1885). These levels include knowledge-of, knowledge-about (also referred to as knowledge-that), and knowledge-how.

Knowledge-of

This entry level of knowing might best be described as an awareness level. Knowledge-of consists of being acquainted with, rather than familiar with a topic. James (1885) referred to this level as "knowledge by acquaintance" to distinguish it from more advanced levels, which he referred to as "knowledge by systematic study and reflection." For example, a "lay" person may be knowledgeable of a field of study called astrophysics and might even know something about what astrophysicists study; however, it would be inaccurate to say that this person is knowledgeable about astrophysics in any way other than on a very superficial awareness level.

Knowledge-of involves remembering (storage of knowledge), recollecting (retrieval of knowledge), and recognizing, but this level does not ordinarily include more advanced processes of the mind. Most curriculum development efforts begin with the knowledge-of level, but proceed quickly to the knowledge-about level because this level represents the systematic study and reflection that James used to distinguish between lower and higher levels of knowing.

Knowledge-about

Knowledge-about represents a more advanced level of understanding than merely remembering or recalling information. Knowledge-about builds upon remembering and recalling, but it also includes more advanced elements of knowing such as distinguishing, translating, interpreting, and being able to explain a given fact, concept, theory, or principle. Being able to explain a given fact, concept, theory, or principle may involve the ability to demonstrate it through physical or artistic performance (e.g., demonstrating a particular dance movement) or through a combination of verbal and manipulative activities (e.g., demonstrating how a piece of scientific apparatus works).

Among the most important decisions a curriculum developer makes is to determine how much knowledge-about to included in a unit, lesson, or lesson segment and the depth or complexity of coverage. It is at this knowledge-about level that learners must begin to deal with the underpinnings of the discipline. In order to move from acquaintance with facts to mental facility and practical use of content in a field, students will need to understand key concepts that organize the discipline, essential principles that govern the concepts, and ways in which practicing professionals in the field do their work. Teachers who do not have an extensive background in the knowledge area in which they plan to develop curricular units will need to acquire the knowledge. They could take formal courses, study the topic independently, or team up with content specialists in the area in which they plan to develop curricular units. A carefully selected introductory college textbook in a content field is usually the most economical way to begin acquiring the knowledge base necessary for curriculum development in a given field.

Knowledge-how

This level of knowing represents types of knowledge that enable individuals to construct their own meanings and make new contributions to their respective fields of study. In the knowledge-how level, a person applies investigative methodology in order to generate knowledge-about aspects of a given field of study. Most knowledge experts consider the appropriate use of methodology to be the highest level of competence in a content field. It represents the kind of work that is pursued by researchers, writers, and artists who are making new contributions to the sciences, humanities, and the arts. It is this level of knowledge that is typically missing from curricular units of instruction, yet it is this level of knowledge that seems to yield the most excitement from students who are placed in the role of "firsthand inquirers" by using the methodological skills of the practicing professional.

These three levels, especially the second and third levels, also exist on a continuum from the simple to the complex. The curriculum developer is responsible for determining the degree of complexity within each level that might be appropriate for a given age or ability group. In the final analysis, it is the curriculum developer's understanding of the content field and instructional techniques plus an understanding of cognitive and developmental psychology that will determine the level of knowledge and content that is appropriate for a particular age group. Much of this understanding comes as a result of experience working with students of varying ages and instructional levels.

In the Multiple Menu Model, the theory of knowledge represented by James' three levels is used in harmony with Alfred North Whitehead's (1929) concepts of romance, technical proficiency, and generalization. For example, according to Whitehead, a young person might develop a romance with (or interest in) the field of medicine while still at the knowledge-of level. This person might pursue the romance (interest) to the point of technical proficiency and become a practitioner in one of the medical professions. Most professionals within a field reach their maximum involvement at the level of technical proficiency, however a few go on to the generalization level. It is these persons who say, in effect, "I want to add new information and contribute new knowledge to the field of medicine." This third level is, in many respects, consistent with one of the major goals of special programming for high ability students.

Selected Concepts From Theories of Curriculum and Instruction

The rationale underlying this model draws upon the work of several other theorists who have made important contributions to curricular and instructional theory, Jerome Bruner and Philip Phenix. Jerome Bruner (1960, 1966) believed that inductive instruction should be the focus of teaching and that content could be taught to any student at any level of development, "that any subject can be taught to any child in some honest form" (Bruner, 1971, p. 71). A major responsibility of the teacher, according to Bruner, is to help the student understand the structure of the subject. This task requires that students learn the fundamental ideas of a subject and how they relate to each other, and he suggested that teachers employ a spiral curriculum to accomplish this goal. In a spiral curriculum, the teacher presents the material at the child's level in an interesting manner. Then as the student moves through the educational process, the teacher presents the same ideas in greater depth and in more complex ways.

Philip Phenix's contributions to curriculum development can be found throughout the Multiple Menu Model. In his work, "Realms of Meaning"

(1964), he addressed the problem of curriculum in light of the "knowledge explosion" and provided four criteria for selecting appropriate content. First, he suggested that content for instruction should be drawn from organized scholarly disciplines or fields of inquiry. It becomes the role of the teacher to mediate the knowledge from these scholarly disciplines so that the knowledge has relevance and meaning for students. Second, Phenix argued that material should be typical and characteristic of the discipline from which it was taken. By selecting content material in this manner, the representative ideas "stand for" large quantities of material, allowing the curriculum developer to be economical in the amount of material selected. The third criterion requires that materials be selected to "exemplify the methods of inquiry in the disciplines" (p. 333). The methods of inquiry or the manner in which practicing professionals in the disciplines create new knowledge defines the discipline. Knowledge and curriculum content are always changing, but the basic means of inquiry change very little. This type of learning leads to a better understanding of the discipline or field of study and also encourages active student participation. Phenix's fourth criterion demands that material be "selected so as to appeal to the imagination of the students" (p. 342). This criterion addresses student motivation and interest. Because students learn best when they want to know, student imagination is the means to make the educational experience meaningful. Thus it becomes important for the curriculum writer to select material and design activities that tap into the interests of the students. Figure 2.1 underscores the importance of appealing to the imagination of students and helps guide curriculum writers as they select course materials and design student learning experiences.

The Multiple Menu Model is also based on the ideas of a group of theorists and researchers including Ausubel (1968), Bandura (1977), Bloom and his colleagues (1954), Gagné & Briggs (1979), Kaplan (1986), Passow (1982), Tomlinson (1999), and Ward (1961). The work of these persons coupled with our own ideas about the process of learning has given rise to this approach to writing curriculum. Except in those instances where specific citations have been made, the work of these theorists is infused in subsequent chapters. Although these writers have influenced the development of the Multiple Menu Model, some of them might disagree with the applications of their work. For example, the Multiple Menu Model relies heavily on Bloom's *Taxonomy* for major sections of the Knowledge and Instructional Objectives Menus (see Chapters 3 and 4), but changes the placement of certain segments in the *Taxonomy*. The largest change deals with the category of Application (Bloom's Level 3.00) which for the purposes of curriculum development and the Multiple Menu Model will be considered a product or outcome of all of the other processes listed in the *Taxonomy*.

Applying Theory to the Construction of the Multiple Menu Model

We developed the Multiple Menu Model as a way for educators to design curricular units that place a premium on both the organization and pursuit of knowledge and the application of investigative methodologies as they pertain to a particular discipline or field of study. It requires teachers to identify a discipline's principles and concepts and to carefully reflect on how they can share the meaning of these ideas with the young people with whom they work. It encourages the curriculum writer to offer students opportunities to apply the research methodologies that practicing professionals use in their fields of study. The curriculum writer needs to consider all of these elements because it helps students develop deep understandings of the subject matter, grounds students' learning in meaningful and authentic contexts, and equips students with the skills used by practicing professionals so they can apply them in learning new information. This type of curricular planning helps students pursue the depth and complexity of a discipline and its content, rather than learning surface-level content knowledge.

Appealing to the Imagination

1. Imagination belongs with the inner life of students and teachers and acts as the power to make education meaningful.

2. Imagination is a manifestation of human freedom in which one is not constrained by biological needs.

3. Imagination is a distinctively human quality of mind and spirit. Imagination is the key to motivation.

4. Imagination is the power that renders experience meaningful. It lifts the learner outside him/herself. The routine, dull, and non-exciting are meaningless.

5. Students learn best when they want to know. Their learning efficiency is in direct relation to their motivation.

6. Materials should be selected in the light of students' real interests.

7. Materials should be selected for its power to stimulate the imagination.

8. Materials should be selected from the extraordinary rather than everyday life experiences.

9. Material should not be bizarre, esoteric, sensational, or full of showmanship.

10. Material should allow the student to see more deeply, feel more intensely, and comprehend more fully.

11. Material should differ according to person, maturity, and cultural context. No materials can be labeled "imaginative" for everyone.

12. Teachers must exemplify an imaginative quality of mind.

13. Teachers must have faith in the possibility of realizing meaning through awakened imagination.

Adapted from Phenix, P. H. (1964). *Realms of meaning.* New York: McGraw-Hill.

Figure 2.1. Guidelines for appealing to the imagination.

Because of the accelerated rate at which knowledge is expanding today, we have organized The Multiple Menu Model to address the selection of content and the selection of procedures in a way that maximizes the transfer of learning to new situations. The model concentrates on the various structural elements of a discipline and focuses instruction on the basic principles, functional concepts (Ward, 1960), and methodologies within that discipline. Teachers should view principles and concepts as tools that help the learner understand any and all of the selected topics of a content field. Information of this type is referred to as "enduring knowledge," as opposed to time sensitive topics or transitory information. For example, understanding the concept of reliability is central to the study of psychological testing; reliability, therefore, may be considered an enduring element of that field. The specific reliability of any given test, however, is more timely or transitory in nature because it changes over time (and from test to test). It is the type of information that learners can always "look up" and understand if they have a basic comprehension of the more enduring concept of reliability.

In a similar fashion, The Multiple Menu Model deals with content selection by focusing on what Phenix (1964) calls representative topics. These topics consist of any and all of the content in a field that the curriculum developer might choose as the focus of a unit, lesson, or lesson segment. For example, a teacher might choose *The Merchant of Venice* as a representative literary selection to illustrate the key concept of a tragic hero. He or she may also integrate other selections that employ this key concept into the unit of study, and a second or third selection might be necessary if an instructional objective is to compare and contrast tragic heroes. It is not necessary to cover an extensive list of selections if one or a few representative literary selections can convey the concept. Similarly, a teacher can cover the biological topic of tropism by selecting phototropism as the major focus of a unit and then making reference to other tropisms (geo-, hydro-, chemo-, and thigmo-) that are based on the same general principle. Students should, of course, have the opportunity to follow up on related topics if they develop an advanced interest.

The Multiple Menu Model emphasizes process objectives that have broader transfer value such as application, appreciation, self-actualization, and improved cognitive structures. In other words, this model views representative topics as vehicles for process development. The structural dimensions and key concepts mentioned above provide the learner with tools for examining any topic in a given discipline. This model views the learner as one who is developing, practicing, applying, and gaining an appreciation of a particular segment of knowledge by studying a representative topic. The student may then use the same strategies to examine other topics.

This model also emphasizes appropriate use of methodology within content fields. All content fields can be defined, in part, by the research methods and investigative techniques that are used to add new knowledge to that field, and most knowledge experts consider the appropriate use of methodology to be the highest level of competence in a content field. Indeed, research scientists, composers, authors, and academicians who are making new contributions to their fields typically operate at this level. Although this level requires an advanced understanding of a field and sometimes requires the use of sophisticated equipment, young students can successfully learn and apply some of the entry level methodologies that are associated with most fields of knowledge (Bruner, 1960). A focus on the acquisition and application of methodology encourages more active learning and an active involvement with a content field.

3

The Structure of the Knowledge Menu

It is best to learn a few concepts well and to know
how to apply them than to cover long lists of topics
for the purposes of recall.

—*John Goodlad*

The Multiple Menu Model (Figure 3.1) provides curriculum developers with a set of practical planning guides or menus to help them in the process of combining authentic knowledge with instructional technique. Just as software programs such as Microsoft® Word present menus to help users create documents, each menu in this model offers a range of options from which the curriculum developer can choose. Each menu represents the knowledge segments that will form the basis for a curricular unit, lesson, or lesson segment and the various instructional techniques that will enable the knowledge to be taught in an interesting and effective manner.

Using the Knowledge Menu

The Multiple Menu Model focuses on inquiry, asking curriculum developers to select the most important concepts and ideas to share with learners. The Knowledge Menu requires educators to examine a discipline from four perspectives: its location and organization within the larger context of knowledge, its underlying principles and concepts, its methodology, and its most representative topics and contributions to the universe of knowledge and wisdom.

These perspectives become the components of the instructional unit. The first three sections or perspectives of the Knowledge Menu are considered "tools." The final section represents the topics within any field to which the tools may be applied as one goes about the process of "studying" a topic.

Section I

Structure of Knowledge: Helping Students Understand the Location, Definition and Organization of a Field of Knowledge

Teachers designing curriculum units based on the Multiple Menu

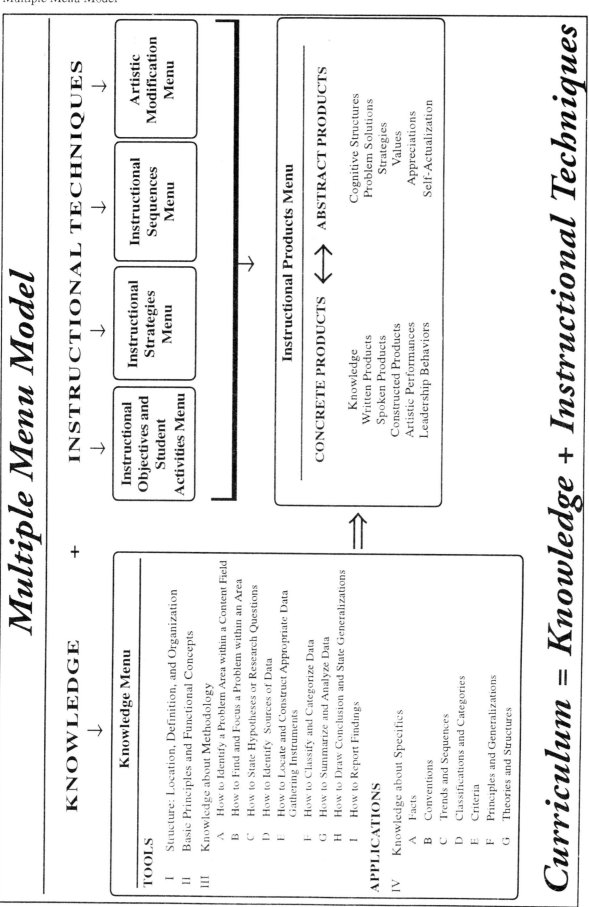

Figure 3.1. Multiple Menu Model.

Model must first locate the targeted discipline in the larger domain of knowledge in order to provide students with an overview of the unique perspectives each discipline or field of study offers in understanding complex phenomena. Next, teachers should examine with their students the characteristics of the discipline and subdivisions to learn why people study a particular area of knowledge and what they hope to contribute to human understanding. This first dimension of the Knowledge Menu helps students examine questions such as "What is sociology?" "What do sociologists study and why?" "How is sociology similar to and different from other disciplines, e.g., psychology and anthropology?" "What, then, is social psychology or social anthropology?" and "How does each fit into the larger picture and purpose of social sciences?" These questions about the structure of the discipline help students gain an understanding of not only where the discipline is located, but also the discipline's connectedness with other disciplines.

Relationships within a discipline and between other disciplines can be best illustrated by using teacher and student graphic organizers, or Knowledge Trees. (Appendix C presents various Knowledge Tree examples.) Curriculum writers can also organize a series of instructional activities that provide an overview and address introductory questions about the specific field of study (see Figure 3.2).

Introductory activities should motivate students to study a particular field and help them develop an interest. For example, in a high school psychology course, an instructor we observed always began the course by showing slides of Sigmund Freud and other early leaders and telling students a few anecdotes related to Freud's most famous cases. This introduction piqued students' interest, and they began to ask inquisitive questions about the information. Similarly, we watched a fourth grade teacher effectively introduce her students to the study of anthropology by bringing in pictures, artifacts, and stories from another culture. She showed a video of a group of cultural anthropologists researching the ways members of a culture view their world. Through the video, she was able to begin exploring the following questions, escalating the level of interest in anthropology and setting the stage for future learning:

- What is human about human beings, and how do we get those qualities?
- What are the common characteristics of different cultures?
- How does the culture change to accommodate different ideas and beliefs?
- What is valued in a culture?

She asked her students to look through the artifacts and speculate on the stories they might tell about a culture and how their own culture tells something about their beliefs, values, and traditions. Eventually, she wanted the students to use the skills of an anthropologist to study a culture and to consider their own culture and how the culture helps define who they are.

The outcome of this particular segment of the Knowledge Menu should lead students into an examination of the questions listed in Figure 3.2 with regard to the specific subdivision of the field being studied. Not every question needs to be explored, nor should this section of the Knowledge Menu necessarily be considered a major focus of the unit of study. Rather, the purpose is to help learners see the "big picture" and the interrelationships that might exist between a field in general and its various subdivisions. This section of the Knowledge Menu is also designed to provide an overview of the field of study. A teacher might deal with Question No. 3 (What are the major areas of concentration of each subdivision?) in a relatively superficial way during the early stages of a unit, but when he or she reaches the last section of the Knowledge Menu (Representative Topics), this topic may become a major area of concentration in the study of a particular subdivision.

The following vignette illustrates how a teacher has used this menu to guide her in the construction of an archaeology unit.

Gail's Journey:
Writing an Archaeology Unit

Gail Pattison created a unit on archaeology for her multi-age 6th, 7th, and 8th grade students. First, she spent time thinking about what she knew about this field. Gail carefully considered how she would introduce the unit to her students and realized that she needed to conduct some research her-

---

Introductory Questions

1. How is this field of study defined?

2. What is the overall purpose or mission of this field of study?

3. What are the major areas of concentration of each subdivision?

4. What kinds of questions are asked in the subdivisions?

5. What are the major sources of data in each subdivision?

6. How is knowledge organized and classified in this field or subdivision?

7. What are the basic reference books in the field or subdivision?

8. What are the major professional journals?

9. What are the major data bases? How can we gain access to them?

10. Is there a history or chronology of events that will lead to a better understanding of the field or subdivision?

11. Are there any major events, persons, places, or beliefs that are predominant concerns of the field, or best-case examples of what the field is all about?

12. What are some selected examples of "insiders' knowledge" such as field-specific humor, trivia, abbreviations and acronyms, "meccas," scandals, hidden realities, or unspoken beliefs?

Figure 3.2. Introductory questions that provide an overview of a field of study.

self. She gathered stacks of textbooks and trade books about archaeology, and she searched the Internet for information about archaeologists. She wanted to know what they did, how they did it, and why. Then she took what she learned and constructed a Knowledge Tree. She felt that this graphic organizer would help her understand how the field was organized and located within the realm of knowledge, and she could then point out the connectedness of the discipline to other fields of study. As Gail learned more about archaeology and its related fields, she constructed two graphic Knowledge Trees (see Figures 3.3 and 3.4) and used them as a starting point for the introduction of her unit. In constructing the teacher Knowledge Tree (Figure 3.3), Gail used Propedias and Macropedias (the last volumes of an encyclopedia) to learn about related fields of study that are interconnected with archaeology. Beginning with the broad disciplines at the bottom of her tree (Math, Science. History and Humanities, Philosophy, Preservation of Knowledge, and Logic), she began to graphically arrange a picture that she could use to introduce students to the field of archaeology. She also created a student Knowledge Tree (Figure 3.4) on which she arranged the broad disciplines at the base of the tree and then graphically illustrated how the top branches of the tree would be explored throughout the unit.

Next, Gail designed a series of introductory lessons to generate an interest in this unit and to provide her students with a global overview of the field of archaeology. Gail decided to start her unit by sharing a personal childhood story with her students:

> As a little girl, I lived with my family in an old house in New England. Part of that house had been built before the Civil War, and there were great nooks and crannies in which to play. But the most intriguing aspect of the house was that it had a secret staircase. (Well I thought of it as a secret staircase.) Before we moved in, a third staircase from the second floor to the kitchen had been boarded up. Upstairs it was a closet and in the kitchen the refrigerator was against that wall. When I found out about this—I was totally mystified! Why would anyone do that, and why wasn't anyone in my family interested in digging into that wall and discovering the old staircase? I was sure that there were things (artifacts) left inside. The workmen could have left old newspapers, coins, tools, etc.
>
> I never was given permission to break in, but it was the stuff of daydreams for years. And I think it was my first brush with the idea of treasures "buried" in an inaccessible place— my imagination.

At this point, Gail brought out an old box. She held it carefully and walked around the room. It was just an old box, but the students saw in Gail's face and through the tender touch of her fingers on the box that this was the stuff of dreams. She then continued her story:

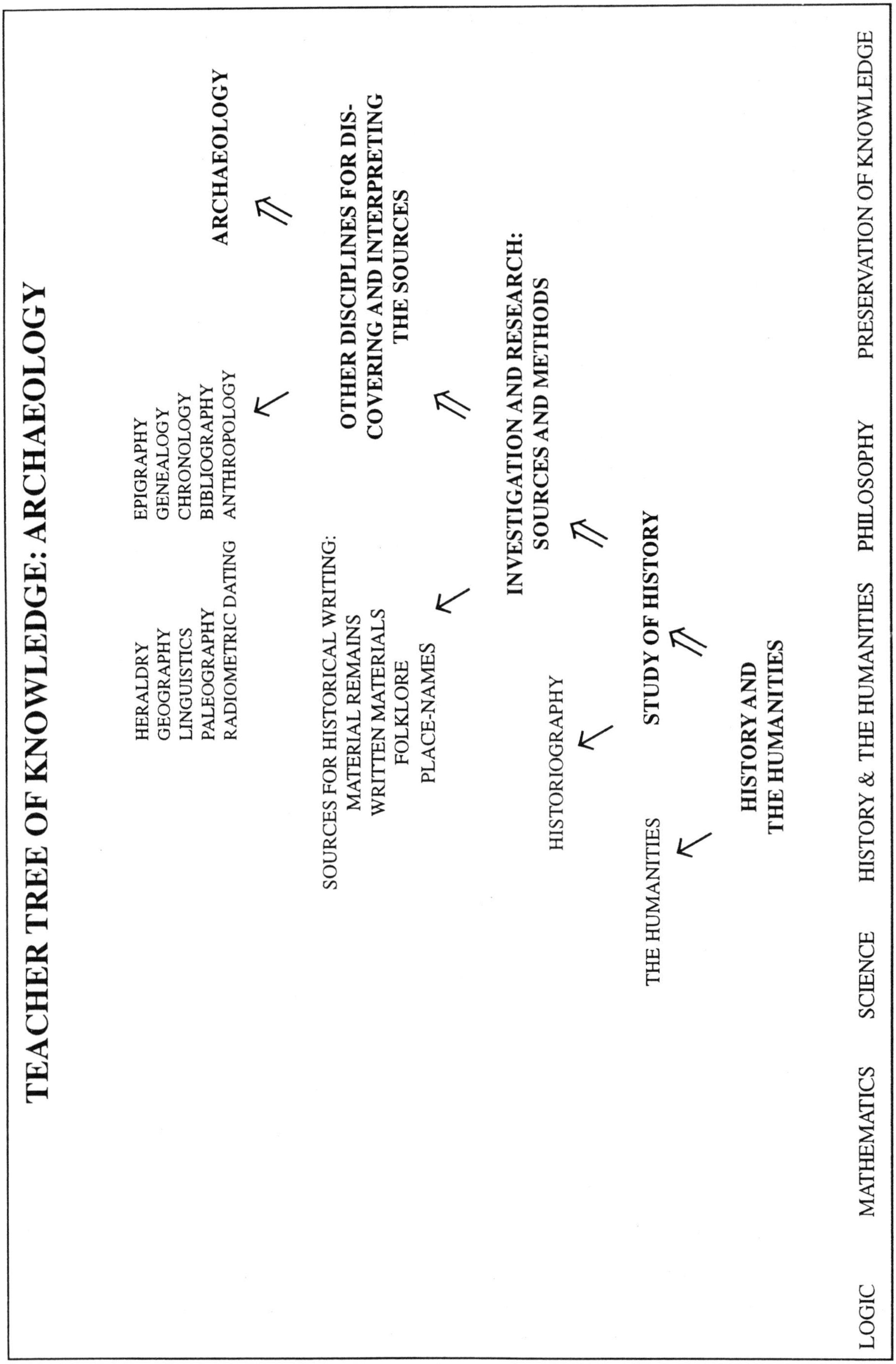

TEACHER TREE OF KNOWLEDGE: ARCHAEOLOGY

ARCHAEOLOGY

EPIGRAPHY
GENEALOGY
CHRONOLOGY
BIBLIOGRAPHY
ANTHROPOLOGY

HERALDRY
GEOGRAPHY
LINGUISTICS
PALEOGRAPHY
RADIOMETRIC DATING

OTHER DISCIPLINES FOR DIS-
COVERING AND INTERPRETING
THE SOURCES

SOURCES FOR HISTORICAL WRITING:
MATERIAL REMAINS
WRITTEN MATERIALS
FOLKLORE
PLACE-NAMES

INVESTIGATION AND RESEARCH:
SOURCES AND METHODS

STUDY OF HISTORY

HISTORIOGRAPHY

HISTORY AND
THE HUMANITIES

THE HUMANITIES

LOGIC   MATHEMATICS   SCIENCE   HISTORY & THE HUMANITIES   PHILOSOPHY   PRESERVATION OF KNOWLEDGE

Figure 3.3. **Teacher Knowledge Tree.**

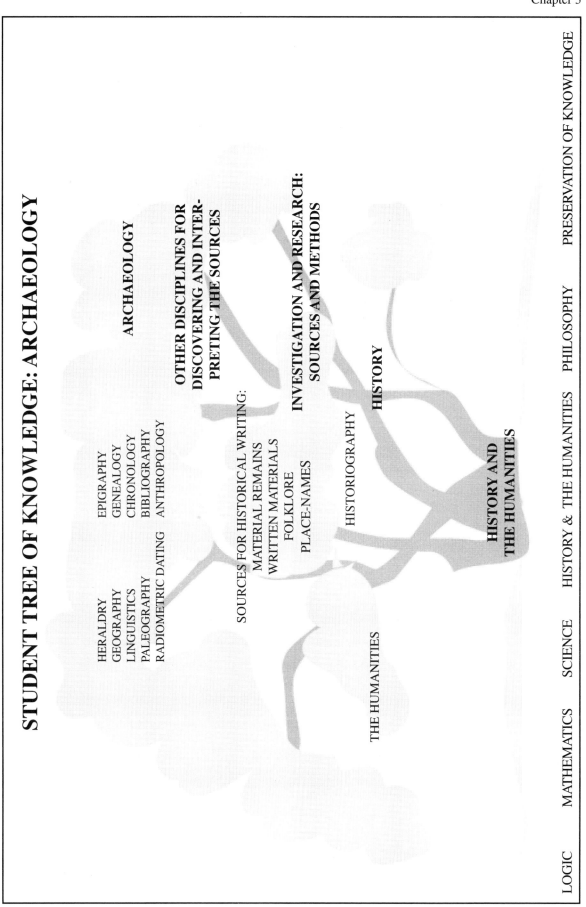

Figure 3.4. **Student Knowledge Tree.**

> *As a child, I used to buy old, ugly, broken pieces of jewelry at rummage sales. I would dig out the colored glass and keep them in a little golden box that looked like a treasure chest. Once, in the fall, I buried the box in the old stone steps behind the barn, and waited until after the last frost in the spring to dig it back up. An archaeological experiment? I think maybe it was.*

In addition to sharing her personal interest in archaeology and showing her students the golden box of jewels that she buried behind the barn, she asked students to compare and contrast her artifact to one they might have. Jack, a tall athletic 8th grader, told about his arrowhead collection. Carol, a quiet 6th grader, fingered the locket around her neck. When asked, she explained that it had been her grandmother's. Inside was her grandfather's picture and a lock of her mother's baby hair. Gail asked her students to consider the following questions: "Could a child in another time period have a similar artifact?" "Have children always had 'treasures'?" and "What do these 'treasures' tell us about someone's culture?"

Now the students were eager to interview their families and search attics and their own rooms for artifacts. Gail started a discussion about the Knowledge Tree to show students where the study of archaeology originates and how other branches of knowledge fit into the study of archaeology. She provided students with a copy of the student Knowledge Tree for their personal reference and continued the discussion by asking her students to brainstorm what they knew about archaeology, checking for prior experience and knowledge of this field of study. In order to help her students understand that archaeological digs not only take place in exotic locations and long ago, Gail saved newspaper articles describing archaeological digs that were local and recent and then asked each student to select an article to share with the others. Gail also decided to create a student-constructed bulletin board containing newspaper articles and a world map to assist her students in locating and recording the digs they read about and to display vocabulary words, career lists, articles about famous archaeologists, definitions, and other student-generated topics.

To provide insight into the work of an archaeologist, Gail selected *Dr. Ruben Mendoza, Archaeologist*, a video from the "Meet the Mentor Series" (Scholastic, 1996). This ten minute interview with a practicing archaeologist set the stage for a live interview with an archaeologist Gail had located at the University of Notre Dame. She asked her students to prepare questions, and, as a group, they conducted a formal interview, photographed the interviewee for their student-constructed bulletin board, and videotaped the interview for future use. Gail also invited her students to think about the many roles archaeologists play as they develop scientific and historical perspectives about an archaeological site.

At this point in the unit, Gail decided to have her students read the prologue of *A Place Called Freedom* by Ken Follett (1995) in which the protagonist finds an iron collar located in a box buried near the remains of an old outhouse on a piece of property he has purchased. After cleaning the artifact, he notices that an inscription becomes visible. Engraved in old-fashioned curly writing, the following inscription emerges: *"This man is the property of Sir George Jamisson of Fife, A.D. 1767."* As the students read the prologue, Gail watched their faces. She noticed her students' eyes widen and then stated, "Archaeology is a science—a science that studies remains. It is also a record of climate, culture, and, most of all, lives. This science has a human side." She had the students ponder several questions: "What if the collar could talk, what kind of story would it tell?" "Where could you find more information about it?" "Who did the collar belong to?" "How could such a thing happen to a human?" and "What might this artifact suggest to us about the belief systems of this culture?"

By considering the organization, location, and definition of the field of archaeology and becoming knowledgeable herself, Gail created a series of lessons that introduced her students to archaeology with a broader sense of understanding. She provided her students with information on how archaeologists define their field, oriented the class to the general purpose or mission of the field, orchestrated experiences that required students to consider how archaeologists carry out their work and what knowledge they pursue, and created interest in the field by sharing personal and related stories that helped students understand why and how individuals become interested in the field of archaeology. Figure 3.5 presents Gail's completed Multiple Menu Unit Plan for Section I of the Knowledge Menu.

With the first part of her unit planning completed, Gail was ready to focus on the next section of the Knowledge Menu: identifying the principles and concepts of archaeology.

Section II

Identifying the Basic Principles and Functional Concepts: Helping Students Get the Big Idea

The second dimension of the instructional unit focuses on identifying and selecting the most important ideas in a particular field of study that need to be explored by the students. Every field of knowledge is built on a set of basic principles and key concepts, and they help facilitate comprehension, information processing, and communication of information that is representative of the essence of the field. These principles and concepts consist of themes, patterns, main features, sequences, and structures that define an area of study. Some of these principles and concepts are applicable to several subdivisions within a given field, but ordinarily the subdivisions have a few concepts that are unique to that branch of knowledge. Indeed, subdivisions of major fields of knowledge probably come into being because of unique concepts (as well as other factors) that result in the establishment of a field's individual identity or a particular subdivision of that field.

Multiple Menu Unit Plan Template

Unit Title **Can You Dig It?   A Study in Archaeology** (Section I: Location, Definition, Organization)   Grade Level **6th-8th**   **Multi-age**

Instructional Objectives and Activities

X Assimilation and Retention

students will

- read articles about an archaeological event to gather details about specific digs conducted throughout the world. Students will record details and descriptions on 3x5 index cards and identify the dig's location on a world map.

X Information Analysis

students will

- select a personal artifact to share with the class. In presentations, students must offer an analysis of what this artifact could reveal about his or her "personal culture" (belief systems, historical significance, etc.)

- analyze a videotape to identify and record vocabulary, concepts, types of research conducted in the field, and personal and professional trait characteristics of an archaeologist (habits of mind). They will include this information in their learning logs.

* (continues on back)

X Information Synthesis and Application

students will

- make plans for producing and hosting the guest speaker event. A final newspaper will be created by the students to share the experience and knowledge gained from the event.

_____ **Evaluation**

Instructional Strategies

X Lecture
_____ Recitation and Drill
_____ Peer Tutoring
X Discussion
_____ Programmed Instruction
X Role Playing
_____ Simulations
_____ Replicated Reports or Projects
_____ Problem-Based
_____ Guided or Unguided Independent Research
X Other   storytelling

Storyboarding the Lessons

The following activities are designed to create an interest in archaeology, introduce basic information about the Knowledge Tree, and provide the teacher with understanding of students' prior knowledge about archaeology.

1. To introduce the unit, gather the students at the back of the room near the display of artifacts and reference materials placed in an interest and learning center that is designated for this archaeology unit. Begin by letting students handle the artifacts. Have them guess what the artifacts were used for and where they might have come from and hypothesize their historical significance.

2. Share my story of when I lived in the old New England house. Return students to their desks and place the "treasure box" on a table for the students to view. Hold up a series of artifacts and pose the following questions: Could a child in another time period have a similar artifact? Have children always had "treasures"? Do these artifacts tell stories? What do these "treasures" help us know about someone's culture?

3. Connect the Knowledge Tree to the discussion by providing an overview of the unit and stating that archaeology is a story of endings. It can be about the death of a city, culture, or civilization. Archaeology is the story of how humankind reveals itself through the things it leaves behind. These artifacts bring archaeologists into intimate contact with a multitude of ordinary, humble people. But the artifact needs to be interpreted. It is through understanding the artifact's purpose, function, and location that researchers begin to see the whole panorama of human development.

** (continues on back)

Instructional Products

Concrete Products

X Artistic
X Performance
X Spoken
X Visual
_____ Models/Constructions
_____ Leadership
X Written

Abstract Products

X Cognitive Development
X Affective

Artistic Modification

- Story of living in an old New England home and finding hidden treasures.

- Bring my collection of archaeology books, articles, reference materials, and videotapes from home for the students to use in their research.

Student Inquiry Questions

1. What is archaeology?
2. How does a culture reveal itself through artifacts? How do cultural artifacts reveal cultural knowledge?
3. How do speculation, probing for historical evidence, and inductive and deductive reasoning play a role in the work of an archaeologist?

Assessment

X Product Assessment
X Interviews/Observations
X Journals
X Learning Logs
_____ Performance Assessment
_____ Oral
_____ Multiple Choice
_____ Essay
_____ Other

Reference Materials/Community Resources

- "Meet the Mentor" videotapes from Scholastic
- A Place Called Freedom (Author Ken Follett)
- Article file on archaeology digs
- Archaeologist from Notre Dame

Figure 3.5. Gail's completed Multiple Menu Unit Plan for Section I of the Knowledge Menu (front).

* **Information Analysis, continued**
  - design an interview protocol to guide the guest speaker interview. The protocol will contain questions in various categories deemed important by the students and teacher. Students will create a recording sheet to record and gather data from the interview.
  - read Ken Follett's *A Place Called Freedom* and speculate on what artifacts might reveal about a particular historical time period, suggest belief systems within a culture, and question whether one source of information provides enough evidence to support a generalization of these data to other cultures or to the whole culture.
  - organize through narrative text and visual illustrations what they have learned from the class activities. Students will create sentence strips that identify specific understandings. They will also respond to a series of teacher-generated journal prompts that probe conceptual understanding of the meaning of culture, belief systems, artifacts, habits of mind, etc. and their relation to each other.

** **Storyboarding the Lessons, continued**
4. Ask students to locate an artifact at home that is particularly interesting to them. They will prepare an oral "artifact story" with the rest of the class. Distribute guidelines that specify what should be included in this oral presentation. As students return to class the next day, they will form groups of five to play "20 questions" to see if they can guess why this artifact may have personal meaning for its owner. They will try to guess its purpose, function, and location.

5. Divide students into teams to read newspaper articles about archaeological digs that have taken place in locations far and near. Students will summarize these articles by noting the details of the dig (where it occurred, the date of the dig, and other details) that reveal an understanding of the article they have read. Students will record the summaries on 3x5 index cards and place them on one of the several bulletin boards that will be devoted to this instructional unit. Students are to identify the location of the dig by using a string of yarn to match the index card to the location of the site on a world map. Hold a discussion to reveal that archaeological digs not only take place in exotic locations and long ago, but also in our own backyards and as recently as a few years ago.

6. Students will then watch a video from the "Meet the Mentor Series" to identify the type of work conducted by archaeologist Ruben Mendoza. In their student archaeology journals, students will record information that describes the work of an archaeologist, the skills that they use to conduct their work, and a listing of words and any definitions that they feel may be helpful in their understanding of the field. They will also look for evidence of the types of dispositions (personal and professional characteristics) or habits of mind that Dr. Mendoza demonstrates as he makes his video presentation. This information will be used as a point of discussion as students form pairs to share the information they gathered. Students will refine this information as they gain a deeper understanding of archaeological principles, concepts, and research methods.

7. To further explore the field of archaeology, a practicing archaeologist from Notre Dame will be scheduled for a class presentation. The students will host this event, with each group of students being assigned a role to play during this presentation. All students will generate interview questions that will help them learn something new about archaeology and its related branches of knowledge. Students will then prepare plans for carrying out the roles they have chosen to play during the interview and presentation. Some of the roles might include students videotaping and photographing the event, rendering artistic displays of the event, gathering a written account for future newspaper articles, or even serving as the moderator during the interview process. Let the students plan this event, specifying their interests and choices in the roles they are to play. Written plans will be requested from the students so everyone is aware of how the day's events will proceed.

8. Distribute copies of the prologue from *A Place Called Freedom* by Ken Follett. After preparing students for this reading, instruct them to "buddy-read" this prologue to identify the types of historical and scientific thinking used by archaeologists to uncover the meaning of this artifact. As they identify these thinking skills, have them describe why and how this thinking would assist in the identification and interpretation of the artifact. Additionally, they will speculate on who the collar might have belonged to and what the artifact suggests to them about belief systems during specific historical times. They will also discuss with one another if it is possible to generalize these belief systems to the whole culture.

9. Students will reflect on these introductory learning experiences (what they have come to understand about the field of archaeology) and record these understandings on sentence strips which will be posted on the bulletin board. To probe their understanding of word definitions, concepts (artifacts, belief systems, cultures), and their relationships to each other, students will also respond to a series of journal prompts using narrative text and graphics.

Figure 3.5. Gail's completed Multiple Menu Unit Plan for Section I of the Knowledge Menu (back).

Basic principles are generally agreed upon truths that have been arrived at through rigorous study and research. Principles are often stated as relationships among concepts, and they concisely summarize a great deal of information (see Figure 3.6) and have the potential to provide information that applies to diverse situations. While these principles can be viewed as "enduring truths," they may need to be modified in the future in light of new evidence. Principles may be factual and concrete (e.g., in order to survive, a civilization must be able to answer the basic biological needs of its members: food, drink, shelter, and medical care) or abstract and open to various interpretations (e.g., each culture views the physical environment in a unique way, prizing aspects of it that may be different from those prized by others). When carefully worded, teachers can use these statements as the organizational framework of a curricular unit. Principles help learners probe the "big ideas" of a discipline and help teachers get to the heart of the content. We have found that when teachers carefully consider these principles as the central organizers of the unit, they are better equipped to explain to students the relevance of the content to their lives.

Functional concepts (Ward, 1960) are the intellectual instruments or tools with which a subject area specialist works. In many ways, these concepts serve as the vocabulary of a field and the vehicles by which scholars communicate precisely with one another. Concepts are powerful organizers of meaning that help label and make sense of large quantities of information within a field of knowledge. Unlike facts, which are limited to specific situations, concepts are broad enough to apply to many sets of conditions. A good way to identify the functional concepts of a field is to examine the glossary from a basic textbook in that field or highlighted words in a teacher's instructional manual. Like principles, there is usually a high degree of general agreement among scholars in a particular field about the meaning of functional concepts. Using principles and concepts as the focus of curricular studies is particularly useful because of the potential they hold for organizing large quantities of information together in some meaningful manner, generating student inquiries (see Figure 3.6) which in turn can lead to enhanced understanding and student involvement, and illustrating the interconnections between and among various disciplines.

In looking at concepts as organizing frames of reference, Brandwein (1987) suggested that when curriculum is developed it should create a plan or a structure for seeking, recognizing, and valuing experience. If constructed correctly, a curriculum helps learners select what is meaningful and useful in their lives. He further explains that the structure of a particular curriculum has at least three characteristics:

1. It has a body of concepts, and these concepts will be useful for recognizing the elements and details of the subject matter.
2. The concepts will control the procedures (or modes) chosen for inquiry.
3. The concepts (and modes) lead to other concepts and modes as learning proceeds.

Field	Basic Principles	Concepts	Student Inquiries
Political Science	Societies establish systems of authority that make decisions and enforce social regulations on members of society.	democracy, monarchy, totalitarian, theocracy, equality, distribution of authority, freedom	What are the various forms of government? Who decides the rules of law? Who enforces these rules? What is the decision making process like in various political systems? How is freedom viewed in various political systems?
Mythology	Throughout the ages, humankind has explained the unexplainable through myths.	phenomena, reasoning, beliefs, storytelling	Why are some myths created? How do myths explain the unexplainable? When does a myth lose it's explanatory power?
Geography	Innovation and change influence the accessibility and desirability of places.	innovation, spatial distribution, density, cultural transmission, region	What changes have affected this community? How is our community different from other communities? Does region and location influence innovation and change? What does it mean to live in a desirable location? How is this decision determined?
Cartography	The environmental and cultural characteristics of people vary according to location.	relative and absolute position, latitude, longitude, prime meridian, equator, environmental interaction, culture	How does location reflect environmental and cultural characteristics of people? Are cultural characteristics shaped by location and place? Which geographical features may hinder the development of a region?
Sociology	Every society develops a system of roles, norms, values, and sanctions that guides the behavior of individuals within society.	roles, values, perception, conflict, norms, discrimination, prejudice	What accounts for differences among people? What elements do different cultures seem to have in common? How do roles, norms, values, and sanctions guide behavior? Is it possible for a diverse society to develop a system which guides the behavior of its members?
History	The history of a culture provides guidelines for understanding the thoughts and actions in the culture's present-day affairs.	change, continuity, chronology, culture	What causes the collapse of a civilization? How do traditions, beliefs, attitudes regulate a culture?
Cytology	The cell is the basic unit of all living organisms.	single cells, multicellular, traits, heredity, mitosis, structure, function, mutations, chromosomes, DNA	How do cells reproduce? What is the difference between those organisms that are single cellular vs. multicellular?
Biology/ Ecology	An organism's pattern of behavior is related to the nature of that organism's environment, including the kinds and number of other organisms present and the availability of food and resources. When the environment changes, some plants and animals survive and reproduce and others die or move to new locations.	biodiversity, interdependent, symbiosis, migrate, hibernation, instinct, homeostasis, mutualism, mutation, adaptation	How do plant and organisms survive in adverse environmental conditions? What occurs when similar organisms compete for resources? Do all organisms adapt in a similar fashion? Are some organisms equipped with better skills of adaptation?
Astronomy	Objects in the sky have patterns of movement.	shadows, cycles, rotation, revolution	What makes a shadow? How do shadow lengths change during the day? How is summer different from winter? What changes as winter gives way to spring?

Figure 3.6. **Examples of basic principles, concepts, and student inquiries.**

Theoretically, this process is never-ending. Brandwein (1987) provides an explanation of how using concepts and principles as the unit's conceptual framework allow for variety, for comparison and contrast, and for exploration and discovery:

> Knowledge is, in a sense, organic: it grows. In the social sciences, for example, there are such major concepts (often called "conceptual themes") as interaction between social groups, market choices in an economy, and resolution of international conflict. Subsidiary and lesser concepts exist, of course. In social interaction, there are subsumed the concepts of group, family, community, leadership, citizenship, and the like. In market economics there is a range of subsidiary concepts, such as gross national product, balance of trade, the cost of production of goods and services and currency. These concepts can be thought of as a shorthand of conceptual language: they are the sentences of conceptual grammar. Thus the concepts of price, goods, and services are linked in the concept-statement: "The price of goods and services in an otherwise unregulated market depends on supply and demand." Such a statement is for common purposes generally "true." In the sciences there are major concepts (or conceptual themes): life, matter, energy, interdependence, and continuity. In the humanities there are truth, beauty, justice, love and faith. These are stated in terms that the teacher grasps immediately. But the child's comprehension and language are, of course, different. (p. 36)

He further explains the difference between constructing curriculum that focuses on topics and those that are designed around conceptual ideas:

> A concept opens up a variety of experience, of intelligible content. It leads to analysis and synthesis. It is not concepts but encyclopedic "topics" that tend to be rigid and confined in sequence. A topic can be "lectured." A concept is "sought" and perhaps "caught" in good time. One can "finish" a topic; a concept grows. In fact, in teaching say history or economics, a topical sequence is extremely rigid,

for it states inflexibly the body of knowledge
that is meant to be "covered." A conceptual
sequence, on the contrary, allows for variety,
for comparison, and contrast, for exploration
and discovery. It depends on problem-posing
that varies within the idiosyncratic modes of
inquiry. (p. 36)

In this section of the Knowledge Menu, curriculum writers determine which basic principles and functional concepts will become the focus of the instructional unit. Teachers must ask themselves important questions as they begin the curriculum planning process: "What is it that I am trying to teach an understanding of? What is it about cultures (for example) that I want my students to understand?" After selecting these principles and concepts, the curriculum writer can then begin to create a series of learning experiences that will help students uncover the meaning behind these conceptual ideas. The learning experiences should motivate students to explore, discover, examine, question, and scrutinize the principles and concepts so that they render meaning for the students; they should not simply mention or cover the concepts in some artificial manner. Developing a unit that has students construct an understanding of a discipline's principles and concepts helps students apply and transfer their understanding to other topics and to other disciplines.

Gail's Journey:
Exploring the Principles and Concepts of Archaeology

As Gail prepared the second section of the Knowledge Menu, she sifted through stacks of old college textbooks, studied the National Council for the Social Studies content standards (NCSS, 1994), and called, wrote, and read works of several working archaeologists. After carefully considering the age level of her students and the time frame available to teach this instructional unit, Gail selected several principles and concepts as the focus for her instructional unit (see Figure 3.7). She then set up a sequence of learning experiences that would help her students uncover the meaning of these conceptual ideas and created situations in which students could apply them to other related topics (e.g., ancient civilizations, American history, etc.). As the students worked through the unit, she wanted them to select civilizations to analyze through the eyes of an archaeologist.

Gail introduced the students to the concept of an artifact by sharing an experience that illustrates the significance of an artifact and the use of archaeological ethics at an archaeological site.

When I was eleven, I went to Europe with my parents
and visited my first excavation. In Rome, we were taken on a
special tour under St. Peter's Cathedral to where archaeolo-
gists had found some of the original catacombs of ancient
Rome. It was a beautiful day in Rome. The sun was shining.

The air was warm. The city was full of people and all the sounds of life—people talking, laughing, cars honking.

Then the tour guide led us around St. Peter's. The world grew quiet and still. As we went down the stairs, the air grew cooler and I shivered. It wasn't just the cold. There was something about this place—something special. Maybe it was all the lives that passed this way so long ago, all the people for whom this was their final resting place.

I remember we were walking down this long hall. I could hear our footsteps, the click of my mother's heels, the slap of my sandals, and the solid thump of Dad's oxfords. I looked up at my dad. His face was glowing. It wasn't the light in the catacombs. It was a light inside him—awe, I think—at being in the presence of so much history.

I stumbled, then tripped on something hard. I looked down and there was a piece of marble, a corner of something—a tomb maybe. I picked it up—that marble corner. It was cool in my hands. It was carved. I ran my fingers over it. I thought of some family long ago who paid to have that carving, paid to make a place beautiful, a place to lay their father. . . .

I slipped it in my pocket and ran to catch up with my mom and dad. I didn't show them what I had. I think I knew they'd make me put it back, but when we got back to the U.S., I gave it to my dad. I saw a little of that light on his face again.

He left that piece of marble on his desk until just recently. It made him think of me, he said, and our times together. [Gail held up the corner of carved marble for all the

---

Archaeology

Principles
- Throughout time, humanity has shared common cultural characteristics.
- Humanity leaves evidence of their common culture in their artifacts.
- The past is revealed through studying the artifacts left by other cultures.
- Archaeology is the detailed, reconstructed story of our shared past conducted by scientists and historians using research methods.

Concepts

• Artifacts	• Documentary Evidence
• Interpretation	• Primary and Secondary Sources
• Culture	• Tradition
• Perspective	• Stratigraphy
• Preservation	• Cultural Variation
• Excavation	

Figure 3.7. Archaeology principles and concepts on which Gail chose to focus her unit.

class to see. She heard murmurs of appreciation.] *I have in my hands, Gail said quietly, an artifact of ancient times, a symbol of a young girl's love, and proof that I committed The Cardinal Sin of Archaeology.*

Gail then asked her students to consider the ramifications of her decision and invited them to explore a series of questions: "How are times different from a dig in the 1950s to a dig in the 1990s?" "What precautions are used today that might not have been employed long ago?" and "How would this artifact assist archaeologists in constructing a story of the past?"

After this discussion, the students worked in groups to generalize about the significance of the types of cultural contributions civilizations leave behind to record their history. Gail asked the class, "What does a culture leave behind so that future generations will know its history and to whom do these artifacts belong?" Gail instructed her students to consider this question, generate a list of artifacts that they might leave behind to represent their local community's history of the 20th century, and explain how they hope their artifacts would be used. After identifying the items, the students categorized the list of artifacts and assigned a conceptual/categorical label to them. The class then shared their responses, and Gail listed the categories on the chalkboard (religious beliefs and practices, government, family, rules, technology, food, shelter, clothing, language, art, music, drama, and games and leisure). Gail asked the students how cultural contributions help explain the story of a civilization and what could be gained from those stories.

In the next series of activities, Gail showed the students a large, closed box with an item rattling inside it and invited the students to think of all the questions they might ask in order to discover what the box contained. She asked one student to type the list of ideas so that students could use the list in the next activity:

- *Where and when was this object made?*
- *Does it have any decorations?*
- *Does it open and close?*
- *What materials were used in the construction?*
- *Where might you find this object? Is it part of a larger object?*
- *What does this object tell you about the people that might have used it?*
- *Is it older than you? your parents? your grandparents?*
- *What can you compare it to?*

To further explore the concept of an artifact, Gail gave her students thirty odd objects, all small enough for the students to handle. She invited them to examine the objects using their list of questions. (Gail obtained these items from an old salvage yard that she had located in her community. With the assistance of the store owner and several other interested customers, she identified each item so that she could share this information with her students.) Following this activity, the students compared their work with that of an archaeologist and explored what these artifacts tell about their culture.

While developing this unit, Gail also created several simulations so the students could apply the inquiry skills used by archeologists at a dig site. In a trash can simulation, students carefully observed and analyzed artifacts deposited in a trash can belonging to an unidentified homeowner, and, based on their observations, drew conclusions about the homeowners.

To help her students understand the idea that archaeologists often have to think like historians and detectives, she located a reference book, *In Search of This and That: Tales from an Archeologist's Quest*, by Ivor Noel Hume (1996). The stories of real archaeological adventures stimulated discussion and speculation on the part of the students. Gail selected the tale, "A Night Remembered: Tainted by the Smoke of Scandal," a story about how archaeologists determined the cause of a fire at an asylum in 1885, to illustrate how, nearly 100 years later, archaeologists used artifactual evidence to reconstruct the past in much the same way that police detectives assemble clues to identify criminals and their crimes. Using artifacts and primary and secondary source documents, the archaeologists put the story together and helped verify speculation and rumor about the events which led up to the fire.

For Section II of the instructional unit, Basic Principles and Functional Concepts, Gail created a series of activities to help her students uncover how archaeologists use physical and documented evidence to reconstruct stories of the past and consider how a culture can be explored through the artifacts it leaves behind. Figure 3.8 shows her completed Multiple Menu Unit Plan for Section II of the Knowledge Menu. She now turned to the third section of the Multiple Menu Model where she considered how to assist students in applying the research methods of the practicing archaeologist.

Section III

Knowledge about Methodology: Helping Students Act Like Practicing Professionals

The third section of the instructional unit focuses on designing instructional activities that engage students in exploring research-based inquiries that are common to a particular field of study (e.g., in a study of plants, activities that lead students to use methods and procedures used by a botanist). There are two types of methodologies: general and specific. The first type deals with the research method used by practitioners in a field to seek answers to their questions and to make contributions to a discipline. Although these methods may vary across disciplines, they generally involve a series of investigative procedures as outlined in Figure 3.9. Although general college level textbooks can be a useful and economical source of information for locating knowledge about the other sections of the Knowledge Menu, we found that information about the research methodologies used in various fields is seldom included in these sources. As a result, we suggest that teachers begin to gather a comprehensive collection of methodological

Multiple Menu Unit Plan Template

Unit Title __Can You Dig It?   A Study in Archaeology__ (Section II: Basic Principles and Functional Concepts)   Grade Level __6th-8th__   Multi-age

Instructional Objectives and Activities

X **Assimilation and Retention**

students will
- read selections from Ivor Noel Hume's book, *In Search of This and That*, to identify the important contributions historical documents offer in archaeological research.

* (continues on back)

X **Information Analysis**

Students will
- discuss and debate the pros and cons of removing artifacts from dig sites. Students will consider the ethical issues that may surface when an artifact is removed.
- classify and label a set of artifacts to reveal categories of information that can describe a culture. Students will use these categories for further research in Section IV of the Multiple Menu Model.

** (continues on back)

X **Information Synthesis and Application**

Students will
- extrapolate data from artifacts presented to them in a simulation in order to create character profiles.

__ **Evaluation**

Instructional Strategies

X Lecture
__ Recitation and Drill
__ Peer Tutoring
X Discussion
__ **Programmed Instruction**
X Role Playing
X Simulations
__ Replicated Reports or Projects
X Problem-Based
X Guided or Unguided Independent Research
X Other Centers, Debate, Shared Inquiries

Storyboarding the Lessons

The following activities are designed to help students understand the key principles, concepts, and skills outlined for the instructional unit. Students will need to explain, interpret, and apply an understanding of these skills and concepts in the activity assignments.

1. Share the story about my first excavation in Rome where I removed one of the artifacts from St. Peter's Cathedral. Ask students to take this artifact. Pose the following questions for students to discuss in small groups: What was wrong with this decision? How do you think this experience would change if I went on this dig today? What precautions are used today that might not have been employed long ago? How would this artifact assist archaeologists in constructing a story of the past? As the students explore these questions, assign one student to serve as group facilitator, one as a recorder of the issues raised, and one who will report a summary of the group's discussion. Students will debate the pros and cons of this issue.

2. Have students work in small groups to generalize about the significance of the types of cultural contributions civilizations leave behind to record their history. Following this brief discussion, distribute to each group an index card with the following question printed on it: What does a culture leave behind so that future generations will know its history, and to whom do these artifacts belong? Ask students to generate a list of artifacts that they might leave behind to represent their local community's history today. Beside each listed artifact, have students identify its cultural contribution.

**** (continues on back)

Instructional Products

Concrete Products
X Artistic
__ Performance
X Spoken
X Visual
X Models/Constructions
__ Leadership
X Written

Abstract Products
X Cognitive Development
X Affective

Artistic Modification

- Story of my trip to St. Peter's Cathedral

- Personal collection of artifacts, videos, photographs, and historical documents

Student Inquiry Questions

1. What are some of the ethical decisions that must be considered when conducting research?
2. What categorical types of artifacts provide information about a culture?

*** (continues on back)

Assessment

X Product Assessment
X Interviews/Observations
X Journals
X Learning Logs
__ **Performance Assessment**
X Oral
__ Multiple Choice
__ Essay
__ Other

Reference Materials/Community Resources

- *In Search of This and That* (Author Ivor Noel Hume)
- Article file on archaeology digs and unusual findings
- Reference materials from historical society
- Videotapes, CD-Roms, Internet Access
- Materials to support centers

Figure 3.8. Gail's completed Multiple Menu Unit Plan for Section II of the Knowledge Menu (front).

* **Assimilation and Retention, continued**
  • View videotapes and search for information on the Web. Encourage students to record interesting procedures and tools used at the dig site and post this information on the bulletin boards.

** **Information Analysis, continued**
  • generate a series of questions to reveal information about mysterious artifacts. They will use these questions at the dig site in Section III of the Multiple Menu Model.

  • extrapolate data from a set of historical documents and discuss their relevancy to archaeological research.

  • design a series of experiments and record their observations to determine how artifacts can be removed from a dig site. They will search the Internet for further information on the types of scientific equipment used during an excavation.

  • use measuring instruments to create a scale drawing of a playground.

*** **Student Inquiry Questions, continued**
  3. When is it necessary for an archaeologist to think like a mathematician, historian, geographer, geologist, or scientist?
  4. What kind of data is used when researching a dig site?
  5. How does the inquiry process assist an archaeologist?

**** **Storyboarding the Lessons, continued**
  3. After identifying the items, have students categorize this list and assign a conceptual/categorical label that describes the set. Have the groups compare their labels with each other and then write these student-suggested categories on the chalkboard. (Possible categories might include religious beliefs and practices, government, family, rules, technology, food, shelter, clothing, language, art, music, etc.) Inform the students that as they explore the field of archaeology, this list of cultural contributions may help them gather insights about a particular civilization. Post these categories on the wall for future reference.

  4. Place an artifact in a large, closed box and show it to the students. Ask students to think of all the questions they might ask in order to discover what the box contains. Record these questions on a tape recorder and have one student transcribed the tape. Questions that may surface include: Where and when was this object made? Does it have any decorations? Does it open and close? What materials were used in its construction? Where might you find this object? Is it part of a larger object? What does this object tell you about the people that might have used it? What can you compare it to? As the students generate these questions, provide them with the answers so they can try to guess what is in the box. Use this activity to discuss the role that the inquiry process plays in the work of an archaeologist. Show how the student-generated questions are similar to those posed by an archaeologist.

  5. To apply this inquiry process, locate thirty odd objects and distribute them to the students. (A good source of objects can be found at an old salvage site located in the community.) Tell them that you found these items in their community, but do not reveal the specific location. Their job is to observe these artifacts, describe the artifact in detail, generate a series of questions that would need to be answered to determine what the item is, and make a guess as to its identity and purpose. Students can create a four-column chart and label the columns accordingly: "Artifact #," "Description of the Artifact," "Questions," and "Guess." Following this activity, invite to class the store owner from the old salvage yard where the items were obtained. He can provide students with additional information about these artifacts. Students will compare their findings with his knowledge of the artifact's purpose and identify. Have students identify potential problems that may occur when an artifact is removed from its location.

Instructional Centers

For this section, set up various centers for the students to explore. Students can rotate through the centers in groups of five. In the centers, students apply skills used by detectives, historians, scientists, geographers, geologists, and mathematicians and begin to consider how these skills and thinking processes apply to archaeological research. Students will keep all assignments and products in their learning logs or posted in the back of the room at the learning center area.

Think Like a Detective: To explore how archaeology is like police work and engage students in deductive thinking, create a simulation called, "Explosion at the Airport." Collect five carry-on handbags and fill each with a variety of items that will help build a profile of its owner. For example, a leather-tooled handbag can be filled with a movie theater stub, female watch, highlighter pen (neon), comb, Band-Aid, penny, safety pin, hairspray, matches from a night spot, sunglasses, pencil, two mismatched earrings, make-up bag, hairclip, Hard Rock cafe pin, candy

Figure 3.8. Gail's completed Multiple Menu Unit Plan for Section II of the Knowledge Menu (back).

wrapper, two business cards (one listing the name of the daily newspaper with an interview date written at the top of the card and one advertising apartments for rent), an advertisement from a teen magazine, a college campus map, and a receipt from a college bookstore. Develop the other four handbags to profile an older woman in her 60s or 70s, a retired older man, an international business man with connections to the military, and a young mother who does not work outside the home and has three children. On a card at the center, create a story that explains that an explosion occurred at their local airport, and, although no one was injured, police are investigating the following five pieces of carry-on luggage which were found near the scene of the explosion but were not claimed. Instruct the students to examine one piece of luggage at a time to develop a character profile of the owner that can assist the police in making an identification. After creating these profiles, students will present their profiles and suggest who might own the bags. Allow time for a lively discussion. Ask students to explain how this simulation is like the work of an archaeologist. Have them explain possible scientific experiments that detectives could conduct to determine the bag's owner.

Think Like a Historian: Students will read In Search of This and That: Tales from an Archaeologist's Quest by Ivor Noel Hume. In pairs, students will read one of the tales and create a book talk to share with their peers. These tales illustrate how physical and documentary evidence give archaeologists clues about where to dig. One story in particular, "A Night Remembered: Tainted by the Smoke of Scandal," illustrates how old written documents can provide artifactual evidence as archaeologists propose new explanations that may refute prior claims.

In a similar activity, distribute a diary entry from a young boy named Jack Randolph. This diary entry includes clues as to the family's eating behavior, childhood games, the location of where the family buried their old dog, and detailed plans for how the family was going to build a fence around the vegetable garden. After reading the selection, students will make a list of all the things they might find if they were archaeologists digging in Jack Randolph's yard. Students will discuss the relevance of historical documents and how they become a source of information for an archaeologist.

Think Like a Scientist: Place in the center the story of how a Roman villa was found in the middle of a cow pasture. Share the pictures, drawings, and report that the Italian Archaeological Society developed. Ask students to brainstorm how physical evidence is located at a dig site. As a simulation, bury some small artifacts (coins, beads, broken shards of pottery) in a shoe box. Challenge students to find ways of uncovering the artifacts without actually digging them up. Using water or blowing on them would replicate erosion, shaking or taping the box would replicate earthquakes. Students will explain the types of experiments they tried and what they discovered in these experiments. At this center, students will learn how to grid a site. Ask students to use the Internet to gain information about the types of scientific equipment that might be used at a dig site.

Think Like a Geographer: At this center, students investigate how geographers look at a land formation as a possible dig site. Student will take on the role of pioneers, moving west to settle a new town. Using large white paper, students will sketch out a diagram of what their town would have looked like in the early 1800s. Using reference materials obtained from the historical society, students will select an area that would be good for settlement. Initially, students pencil in basic land formations and locate natural resources such as lumber and water. Students decide where to locate homestead sites and consider where public buildings and businesses might be placed. As they make firm decisions, the students go over these drawings with ink or magic marker.

To symbolize the passing of 200 years, shifting winds, and blowing soil, place brown paper over the first drawing of the settlement. Students now assume the role of a team of archaeology students working with grant money to find the site of an old settlement. As they approach from the east, just as they did as settlers, what can they expect to find? Students redraw the scene after a discussion of how landforms and natural resources change (forests grow, river beds change, etc.). They should consider the following questions: Why might a settlement be abandoned? What kinds of disasters cause families to abandon an area? Is this true throughout history? Can you think of any locations in your community that might serve as a dig site? What would be some visual clues that would indicate these possibilities? How could these visual clues be recorded? At this center students also will indicate how to photograph a site.

Thinking Like a Geologist: For this activity, use a worksheet that shows how layers of soil build up over time. On this worksheet, show pictures of artifacts within four layers of soil. Date these layers 1600-1700, 1701-1800, 1801-1900, 1901-2000. Students must study the layers and the evidence that has been left behind by the people who lived during each particular time period. They then write a paragraph in which they describe and justify what they think the property was being used for while each layer was formed. To add to their knowledge of specific techniques archaeologists use to gather data at a dig site, students will access teacher identified websites to explore stratigraphy, radiocarbon dating, chronology, dendrochronology, and other terms which were introduced to them by the visiting archaeologist from Notre Dame. They will record this information in their learning journals.

Thinking Like a Mathematician: Students pretend that the location for a dig site is approximately the same measurement as the school playground. To learn how to scale, students use a meter wheel to draw to scale an area of the playground. Students use their mathematical skills to make their sketches on a piece of graph paper.

Figure 3.8. Gail's completed Multiple Menu Unit Plan for Section II of the Knowledge Menu (back cont.).

Procedural Steps

1. Identify a problem with in a content field.

2. Find and focus a problem within an area of study.

3. State hypotheses of research questions.

4. Identify sources of data.

5. Locate and construct appropriate data gathering instruments.

6. Classify and categorize data.

8. Summarize and analyze data.

9. Draw conclusions and state generalizations.

10. Report findings.

Figure 3.9. The procedural steps of research methodology.

resource books, sometimes called how-to books (e.g., how to conduct a science experiment, how to conduct oral histories) that can be used to teach students the skills necessary for acquiring knowledge about a specific field's methodology. (See Appendix D for a listing of how-to resources.) Other useful sources of information are laboratory manuals that frequently accompany college level textbooks.

The second type of how-to methodology is more domain specific and assists the researcher in completing the more comprehensive tasks outlined above. For example, a student might learn how to conduct a survey in order to locate and construct appropriate data gathering instruments needed for a research study. Specific examples of methodologies from a number of different fields of study are presented in Figure 3.10.

This section of the Knowledge Menu is especially important for curriculum development because it affects the more active kinds of instructional techniques a teacher can select to use in his or her unit. By providing students with the know-how of investigative methodology, teachers increase the probability of more inductive or "hands on" learning experiences. Once students have learned basic information about a field or topic and the proce-

Field	Methodology
Astronomy	How to chart star patterns using photography
Archaeology	How to grid a dig site
Psychology	How to chart, journal, and interpret dreams
Photography	How to construct a pinhole camera
Philately	How to interpret stamp authenticity and value
Botany	How to identify a tree's age
Cartography	How to use a compass and the sun's position to determine directionality
Cytology	How to prepare a slide
Sociology	How to conduct a survey
Art	How to paint and draw what one sees
Cinematography	How to produce a video
History	How to obtain biographical data through interviews
Communication	How to give a persuasive speech

Figure 3.10. Domain-specific methodologies.

dures for doing some kind of research related to that topic, they can proceed to the application level—the level considered by many to be the highest level of involvement in a field of study. Student investigations may be limited in scope and complexity, and they frequently may follow prescribed scenarios such as the ones typically found in laboratory manuals or how-to books. Nonetheless, including even junior level investigative activities in curricular materials forces teachers to go beyond the omnipresent didactic mode of instruction that has been the subject of so much criticism of education (Goodlad, 1984).

What is asked of teachers in this section is to design learning experiences that will engage students in the methodologies of the discipline being studied. Teachers who write their instructional units using this model will explain, illustrate, and involve students in the process of research as defined by the methodology dimension of the Knowledge Menu (e.g., identify a problem area in the study of archaeology, focus the problem, state an hypothesis, locate resources, classify and organize data, draw conclusions, report findings) and/or create situations for students to apply the domain-specific methodologies to acquire new information. These clusters of diverse methodological procedures that surround the acquisition of knowledge—that dimension of learning commonly referred to as "process" or thinking skills—should themselves be viewed as a form of content. It is these more enduring skills that form the cognitive structures and problem solving strategies that have the greatest transfer value. When teachers view process as content, they avoid the artificial dichotomy and the endless arguments about whether content or process should be the primary goal of learning. Combining content and process leads to a goal that is larger than the sum of the respective parts. The goal is to place students in situations in which they acquire, manage, and produce information in an organized and systematic fashion by applying the thinking and research processes that are used to create this knowledge in the first place. We believe that when students are armed with the tools learned in the Knowledge Menu and have acquired a more mature understanding of the methodology of the field, they are no longer passive recipients of information; they are able to begin the process of gaining and then generating knowledge within the field.

Gail's Journey:
Engaging Students in the Methodologies of an Archaeologist

For this third section of the Knowledge Menu, Gail decided that she wanted her students to experience firsthand what it felt like to be an archaeologist. To carry out this goal, she combed her community surroundings looking for a potential archaeological site:

Over the years of living in Northern Indiana, I have
noticed many foundations of buildings on farm land. One
site seemed particularly useful, and I went to ask the near-

est homeowners if they had any idea who owned the property. While driving up their driveway, I noticed an even better site to the right of their property. When I spoke with the homeowner, he was pleased to announce the land was his, and he gave permission for a dig site preparation. He told me that any artifacts that students found could be taken off the premises and examined. He gave me a history of the area and the site. The site was very overgrown, in a bit of a valley and showed only a stone foundation, approximately seven feet high, with some window wells and door frames. The owner said it had been a "hill barn" built in 1871. (Hill barns are built into the side of a hill or with an artificial hill on one side so that the barn operates on three levels. The lower level were stalls, the middle level, with access on the hillside, was for storing carriages, farm equipment, and wagons, and the top level was a hay loft.)

After teaching her students the methodological skills of how to measure, photograph, and graph a dig site and how to use data recording forms, the students were prepared to visit the site. Equipped with cameras, their recording sheets, and equipment such as trowels and whiskbrooms, the class surveyed the area. Upon returning to their classroom, the students wrote accounts of this experience, describing what they had done, what they had learned, and how they would do it differently the next time. They compared all their drawings and measurements with each other to check for accuracy. They prepared final drawings to scale and completed forms for a classroom display.

To follow-up this experience, the students decided to prepare a similar simulation for other sixth-grade students. They placed artifacts found on their site in three large boxes and buried them in dirt for the other students to discover. Additionally, Gail's class prepared a brief presentation about archaeology and debriefed the students who were engaged in the simulated dig.

This experience provided an opportunity for the students to apply the skills used by archaeologists, and more importantly, Gail knew that this experience might possibly lead to some of her students identifying future interest-based independent studies. Gail's completed Multiple Menu Unit Plan appears in Figure 3.11.

Section IV

Knowledge about Specifics (Representative Topics): Helping Students Apply Basic Principles and Concepts

The fourth section of the unit focuses on the last dimension of the Knowledge Menu and encompasses the main body of knowledge that makes up the content of any given field. In this section, teachers will

Multiple Menu Unit Plan Template

Unit Title Can You Dig It? A Study in Archaeology (Section III: Knowledge About Methodology)

Multi-age
Grade Level 6th–8th

Instructional Objectives and Activities

Assimilation and Retention

___

X **Information Analysis**

Students will

- record, analyze, and summarize their findings from their research in the field.

X **Information Synthesis and Application**

Students will

- create a plan for conducting the dig. They will complete planning sheets to identify equipment needs and assign job responsibilities to various students.

- construct a dig-in-a-box and host a simulated dig for other students. As a part of this preparation, the class will create a training module to introduce these outside students to the field of archaeology and archaeological research.

* (continues on back)

Evaluation

___

Instructional Strategies

___ **Lecture**
___ **Recitation and Drill**
X **Peer Tutoring**
X **Discussion**
___ **Programmed Instruction**
___ **Role Playing**
X **Simulations**
___ **Replicated Reports or Projects**
___ **Problem-Based**
X **Guided or Unguided Independent Research**
X **Other** Audiovisual Presentation, Demonstrations, Field Trip

Storyboarding the Lessons

The following activities are designed to take students onto a dig site to conduct fieldwork. By using the tools and research methods learned in Section II, students will be able to see how archaeology is a detailed, reconstructed story of the past. Students will have an opportunity to apply scientific and historical perspectives as they examine the site.

1. To introduce this section of the unit, share my two stories of how I have found archaeological sites in Italy and in our community. Explain to the students that being observant during site visits may yield some interesting finds.

2. Prior to the actual dig, students will spend a whole day at the archaeological site to determine which locations of the site will be excavated by the students. During this visit, students will identify their equipment needs, develop the types of forms to record data, and develop an organizational plan to determine which jobs will be carried out by different teams of students. Students will take preliminary photographs at the site to assist in locating artifacts and identify-ing specific locations where potential artifacts may be found.

3. On the day of the dig, various groups of students will be in charge of measuring, photographing, graphing, drawing, and writing detailed descrip-tions of the site and any artifacts found during the fieldwork. (All of these skills were introduced in Section II of the Multiple Menu unit as students rotated through the centers or as the students gathered information from the Internet.) Students will be allowed to bring artifacts back to the classroom (permission has been granted to remove these artifacts from the premise) where they will try to identify what they are and what purposes they might have served. Have students write accounts of this experience describing the type of work they conducted, what they learned from this experience, and what changes they would make to their plans. They will share their findings with members of our community Historical Society.

*** (continues on back)

Instructional Products

Concrete Products

Artistic
X Performance
X Spoken
X Visual
X Models/Constructions
X Leadership
X Written

Abstract Products
X Cognitive Development
X Affective

Artistic Modification

- Share story of house in Italy located beneath a castle. The caretaker for the castle kept a small herd of goats which frequently got through the fence and into our yard. One day as my husband and I were looking for the downed fence, we came upon a dim pattern of a mosaic floor. Later we had this ruin confirmed as an official site by the Historical Society in the town of Gaeta. (Show my pictures and draw diagrams on the chalkboard.)

** (continues on back)

Student Inquiry Questions

1. What must be considered prior to the dig taking place?
2. Why is it necessary to plan for a dig?
3. What kind of data do we want to gather at the site?
4. How does recording data assist the archaeologist?
5. What kinds of analyses can be performed on the data?

Assessment

X **Product Assessment**
___ **Interviews/Observations**
___ **Journals**
___ **Learning Logs**
X **Performance Assessment**
___ **Oral**
X **Multiple Choice**
___ **Essay**
X **Other** Article for publication

Reference Materials/Community Resources

- Historical Society
- Archaeology reference books

Figure 3.11. Gail's completed Multiple Menu Unit Plan for Section III of the Knowledge Menu (front).

* **Information Synthesis and Application, continued**
  * present their research findings to our local Historical Society for evaluation and feedback.
  * write feature articles that explain the meaning behind the four key principles identified for this instructional unit. Encourage students to submit their articles for publication.

** **Artistic Modification, continued**
  * Videotape of an archaeologist whom we interviewed during a visit to a dig site in Alaska.
  * Description of how I located an archaeological site for excavation.

*** **Storyboarding the Lessons, continued**

4. Students will analyze the data that they have collected and compare it with each other for accuracy. Using reference materials and community resources, students will try to identify the artifacts. They will prepare final scale drawings and complete forms for a classroom display. Students will present their findings to various classes and to the local Historical Society to explain what they found at the site.

5. Ask students to consider how they can provide a similar experience for other students in their school. Using three large wooden-constructed boxes, invite students to prepare a simulated dig in a box for 150 students. Purchase soil and have students bury artifacts at various layers to approximate an actual dig. The students will create six-grid areas in the box and prepare a recording form to document the location of the buried artifacts.

6. Students will make overview presentations and provide a follow-up question and answer period for the students who will participate in the simulated dig experience. Students will rotate into the simulation in groups of five and then return to the classroom for a question and answer session.

7. At the conclusion of these activities, students will write and submit for publication articles that explain the meaning behind the four key principles identified for this instructional unit. Students can use any of their research findings, experiences, and photographs to illustrate these ideas.

Figure 3.11. Gail's completed Multiple Menu Unit Plan for Section III of the Knowledge Menu (back).

help students apply the "tools" from Sections I, II, and III to selected representative topics in order to acquire an understanding of a specific discipline's content. Unlike traditional instruction, which asks teachers to cover an entire text by the end of the year or semester, the Multiple Menu Model asks teachers to winnow out from all the possible topics in a field the few that truly represent the field's principles and concepts. By narrowing the scope of information to be taught and selecting representative topics, a teacher can focus on finding interesting and dynamic issues that maximize student interest, motivation, and enthusiasm about a particular field of study. For example, there are thousands of studies in psychology that deal with principles of animal learning, but an unusually interesting study (e.g., Skinner's famous experiments on classical conditioning with pigeons) might have more motivational power than less dramatic studies, especially if presented through an engaging film or demonstration. Figure 3.12 presents specific examples of representative topics for various fields of study.

"Knowledge About Specifics" provides a vast warehouse of information from which selected aspects of content may be drawn and to which the "tools" can be applied. The subcategories listed under "Knowledge About Specifics" in Figure 3.13 are based on the first level of Bloom's *Taxonomy* (1954). This analysis of the various ways in which knowledge is organized is helpful in identifying organized components of a particular field. When examining a content area for curriculum development, it may not always be easy to classify a topic according to the subcategories listed in Figure 3.13. For this reason, curriculum developers should consider selecting content based on the ways in which topics are organized in standard (college level) text and reference books. After a teacher has developed a unit, he or she should review the material in an effort to identify facts,

Field	Representative Topics
Botany	Applying the principles of botany in understanding the problems of deforestation in the rain forests.
Geography	Applying the concept of regionalization to world geography or world history. In history, students can apply the concept of regionalization in analyzing the South, or students can apply the concept of regionalization and its effect on voting behavior in a particular area.
Mythology	Exploring how various myths (from various cultures) and descriptions of their main characters reveal cultural belief systems of the past that were largely mysterious.
Cytology	Applying knowledge of the principles and concepts of cells to engage in debates on genetic testing, closing, mutations, etc.
Microbiology	Examining the relationship between the dumping of animal waste and the healthiness of a stream.

Figure 3.12. Examples of representative topics.

A.   Knowledge about Facts

This category includes knowledge about dates, events, persons, research findings, and terminology. Information such as time periods in history or ages in paleontology would also be included in this category. Knowledge about Facts might include single circumscribed bits of information (e.g., the date of the battle of Lexington and Concord) or entire chains of events (e.g., the chronology of the battles of the Revolutionary war). Also included in this category is knowledge about sources of information, particular books, data tables, and compilations of facts associated with various fields of study.

B.   Knowledge about Conventions

This category includes rules, formulas, common symbols and representational devices (e.g., the symbols used on a weather map), and the forms that are commonly used to represent work in a particular field (e.g. verse, narrative, story boarding, scientific papers). The rules of grammar, usage, punctuation, and spelling for written and spoken language is a good example of Knowledge about Conventions.

C.   Knowledge about Trends and Sequences

This category represents interrelationships between and among specific pieces of information in a field. The relationships may be temporal or chronological (e.g., the sequence of events in a plant's reproduction cycle), but in almost every case knowledge about trends and sequences involves some types of causal relationship. Thus, for example, plant reproduction, stock market increases, or a decline in the infant mortality rate can usually be studied from a cause and effect perspective. Some trends and sequences might be based on direct, obvious, and factual relationships, or they might be complex, subtle, and open to many different interpretations.

D.   Knowledge about Classifications and Categories

This category deals with grouping information according to various elements of commonality. In many cases, these categories serve as the bases or organizational theme through which a topic can be studied in a systematic matter. Types of literature, forms of government, and classes of plants or animals are all examples of how information is classified for more organized study and ease of understanding. Classifications and categories are extremely useful tools in helping students manage large amounts of information, and they also help facilitate meaningfulness between and among individual pieces of information by calling attention to common characteristics, themes, or structures.

E.   Knowledge about Criteria

This category deals with the quantitative and qualitative standards by which information, objects, or events are judged. Quantitative (i.e., numerical) standards are usually easier to learn than qualitative criteria. Thus, it is far easier to teach students to judge a poet by the number of publications than by the quality of an individual work. Qualitative analysis represents extremely mature levels of development in any field. Curriculum developers should devote some attention to providing students with knowledge about criteria (both quantitative and qualitative) even if they do not expect entry level students to engage in sophisticated judgments. For example, younger students might be made aware of various criteria by which literary material is accepted for publication, even if their present level of development does not allow them to make sophisticated judgments. Knowledge about criteria is always the beginning point for more sophisticated applications that take place at a later point.

F.   Knowledge about Principles and Generalizations

This category deals with the major ideas and broad abstractions that help to summarize and organize large quantities of information about a given discipline. Typically, they include abstract statements that help to explain, describe, predict, or determine the most appropriate and relevant action or direction to be taken. Principles and generalizations become the organizational structures under which specific facts and events can be placed and assist students in seeing the "whole picture" of a particular phenomena. For example, in geography, there are many principles and concepts that geographers consider important (i.e., the location of an area in relation to other places helps to explain its pattern of development; the character of a place is not constant—it reflects the place's past, present use, and future prospects). The challenge to the teacher is to identify the principles and concepts that become the foundation for the curricular units they are writing. This foundation helps set the stage for determining how they will assist their students in uncovering what is meant by these statements of relationship among concepts.

G.   Knowledge about Theories and Structures

This category deals with the interrelationships between a body of principles and generalizations which are interrelated to form a theory or structure. When teachers ask students to explain the structure and organization of Congress or even the local city government, they are asking students to explain how various governmental systems interact, what their main purpose is, and how these systems help citizens accomplish a particular goal. The explanation of the structure requires that students reach a level of sophistication in organizing this information to illustrate a complete understanding of this concept called government. Knowledge of theories and structures is the most abstract formulations about a particular phenomena.

Figure 3.13. Knowledge about specifics.

conventions, trends, and sequences. The teacher should call these subcategories to the attention of students, either through direct instruction or by asking them to analyze material according to the ways in which "Knowledge About Specifics" are classified.

The following example illustrates how a teacher used this dimension of the Multiple Menu Model in a literature course. This teacher explored a concept in literature—the genera of tragic heroes—through intensive examination of three prototypical examples (e.g., *The Merchant of Venice*, *Joan of Arc*, and *The Autobiography of Malcolm X*). Selecting more than a single exemplar of the concept allowed for both in-depth analysis and opportunities for students to compare and contrast authors' styles; historical perspectives; ethnic, gender, and cultural differences; and a host of other comparative factors that single selections would prohibit. The aim of the instruction in the beginning stages of the unit was to assist students in understanding the concept of the genera of tragic heroes and why it was being studied. One of the main purposes of the first three sections of the Multiple Menu Model is to learn *how* to study tragic heroes; therefore *who* should be studied (i.e., which tragic hero) was less important as long as the hero was representative of the genera. An emphasis on *how* rather than *who* also legitimized a role for students. The payoff as far as transfer was concerned was to follow up the in-depth coverage with more advance learning that focused on factors that define the concept of tragic heroes (e.g., characteristics, themes, patterns, etc.).

To continue to build this cognitive understanding of the Tragic Hero and to apply literary analysis skills, students formed small interest groups to compile categorical lists and biographical summaries of tragic heroes in sports, politics, science, civil rights, religion, the women's movement, arts and entertainment, and other areas in which students expressed special interest. It is in these small groups that students began to understand the concept in literature known as the genera of tragic heroes.

Once students learned how to analyze a particular genus and after they explored categorical representatives of the genus, students may show an interest in exploring this area in greater detail (i.e., investigating the lives or exploits of tragic heroes and heroines). The beauty of this approach is that students first gain the "tools" for studying a topic; they can then apply those tools to their own interest area.

Gail's Journey:
Exploring Representative Topics

In thinking about "Knowledge of Specifics," Gail knew that the possibilities were endless. In history, the students were required to learn about ancient civilizations, but curriculum guidelines did not state specifically how the students needed to learn the material. Through her assessments, she ascertained that the students understood the importance of the work of an archaeologist, had learned valuable how-to skills during the dig at the farm site and the classroom simulation, and were beginning to ask many questions about the discoveries of ancient ruins, the people, and their way of life. She decided to create a learning experience for the students to examine three major civilizations that were part of the curriculum (Greek, Mayan, and Egyptian). Students signed up in groups and selected one civilization to research. Gail asked them to identify its distinguishing characteristics (people, language, beliefs, values, governmental and social structure, traditions, ceremonies, location, etc.) and to compare these characteristics with the other two civilizations. The students identified categorical questions to direct and focus their research. Some of these questions included:

1. How did this society provide for the basic biological needs of its members (food, shelter, drink, medical care)?
2. How did this society provide for the production and distribution of goods and services (division of labor, rules concerning property and trade, ideas about the role of work)?
3. How did this society provide for the reproduction of new members and laws and issues related to reproduction (regulations, marriageable age, number of children)?
4. What type of training (education, apprenticeship, passing on of roles) was provided to the individual members of this society?
5. How did this society maintain internal and external order (law, courts, police, wars, diplomacy)?
6. How did this society provide meaning and motivation to its members?

Students were required to use multiple resources in their research. Gail encouraged them to use books, Internet sources, films, magazine articles, e-mail exchanges with various on-line archaeologists, as well as their textbook. Gail also contributed her personal collection of resource materials which provided invaluable information gathered from archaeology journals, museum visits, and her travels abroad.

After each group gathered the information on its civilization, they compared and contrasted the information. In small groups, students sat with each other to create diagrams and pictures to illustrate these comparisons across civilizations. Gail instructed them to consider the relevancy of any of the cultural characteristics on modern civilization. Gail asked, "What causes the collapse of a great civilization? What are the prerequisites for the survival of a civilization? What types of questions are the archaeologists trying to answer about the civilization that you studied?"

After this intensive analysis, Gail decided to allow her students to choose how they wished to use the information they had gathered in this unit. Some students considered writing a book to introduce the concept of cultures. These students joined with one other student who was a highly skilled artist to create a children's book that compared the civilization they studied to today's American civilization. Another group decided to research the laws regarding the destruction of archaeological sites and prepare an editorial for the paper. Still others decided to create multimedia presentations about the ancient civilization they studied (HyperStudio projects, Webquests), while others decided to create of a school-wide time capsule, interviewing students in the schools as to those artifacts they considered important representative items reflecting their current culture. One student became interested in providing an historical account of the archaeological dig site that initially was the simulated dig. To assess the products, Gail worked individually with the students to design rubrics that would help them construct their products and identify how the essential understandings (concepts and principles of the unit) would be illustrated in the products they had selected. Figure 3.14 displays Gail's completed Multiple Menu Unit Plan for Section IV of the Knowledge Menu.

Multiple Menu Unit Plan Template

Unit Title __Can You Dig It?__ A Study in Archaeology (Section IV: Representative Topics)

Multi-age

Grade Level 6th-8th

Instructional Objectives and Activities

__X Assimilation and Retention__
Students will
• read various reference books and search the Internet to gather information regarding the civilization they are studying. Students will group the information into categories.

__X Information Analysis__
Students will
• compare and contrast various civilizations based on categories of information gathered in their research.

__X Information Synthesis and Application__
Students will
• create a product which demonstrates an understanding of the key principles, concepts, and skills identified for this instructional unit.

__X Evaluation__
Students will
• generate a set of internal criteria to judge the quality and sustainability of the civilization they have researched.

Instructional Strategies

___ Lecture
___ Recitation and Drill
___ Peer Tutoring
_X_ Discussion
___ Programmed Instruction
___ Role Playing
___ Simulations
___ Replicated Reports or Projects
___ Problem-Based
_X_ Guided or Unguided Independent Research
___ Other

Storyboarding the Lessons

The following activities are designed to have students transfer the knowledge and skills they have acquired through previous work and apply them toward investigations and project work.

1. To introduce this section of the unit, share my Lewis and Clark story to illustrate how research questions can be used to guide the inquiry process.

2. Explain to the students that they will have an opportunity to explore many of the questions they have generated about the discoveries of the ancient ruins they have read about, its people, and their way of life. Divide the class into three groups and ask each group to select and examine one of three major civilizations (Greek, Mayan, and Egyptian) that are part of their studies in the middle school. They will identify its distinguishing characteristics (people, language, beliefs, values, governmental and social structures, traditions, ceremonies, etc.) and compare these characteristics to the other civilizations. They will focus their research on the student inquiry questions and other interest-based questions. Invite students to gather data from books, Internet sources, primary documents, articles, videotapes, films, e-mail exchanges with various on-line professionals, as well as their textbook. After each group has gathered the information on its civilization, students will compare and contrast the information and create diagrams and pictures to illustrate these comparisons across civilizations. Students will identify causes for changes that took place in the civilization over time and explore the question: What are the prerequisites for the survival of a civilization? Students will develop a set of criteria (based on a discussion of this question) to evaluate the quality and sustainability of the civilization they researched.

** (continues on back)

Instructional Products   Note: These products will vary according to student interest.

__Concrete Products__
_X_ Artistic
_X_ Performance
_X_ Spoken
_X_ Visual
_X_ Models/Constructions
_X_ Leadership
_X_ Written

__Abstract Products__
_X_ Cognitive Development
_X_ Affective

Artistic Modification

Describe my impressions of traveling along the Lewis and Clark Trail, culminating with a visit to the Lewis and Clark Interpretive Center in Great Falls, Montana. This story illustrates how research becomes an important method in answering perplexing questions. After stopping to read historical markers on our trip and discovering that members of the expedition ate dog meat to survive, I made every effort to find out about the dogs used in the expeditions and if any survived. I was able to obtain answers to my questions by reading excerpts from the journals of Lewis and Clark.

Student Inquiry Questions

1. How do societies provide for the basic biological needs of its members?

2. How does the society I have chosen to investigate provide for the production and distribution of goods and services?

* (continues on back)

Assessment

_X_ __Product Assessment__
_X_ Interviews/Observations
___ Journals
___ Learning Logs
_X_ __Performance Assessment__
___ Oral
___ __Multiple Choice__
___ Essay
_X_ __Other__ Article for publication

Reference Materials/Community Resources

• Books on various civilizations
• Publication guidelines

Figure 3.14. **Gail's completed Multiple Menu Unit Plan for Section IV of the Knowledge Menu (front).**

student Inquiry Questions, continued
3. Does this society have laws which regulate its population?
4. How did this society educate its people?
5. How did this society maintain internal and external order?
6. How did this society provide meaning and motivation to its members?

storyboarding the Lessons, continued
3. Students will choose how they wish to communicate the understandings, concepts, and skills they have gathered in this unit. Students should look at the products list to identify unusual ways to communicate their new understandings. Individual or group rubrics will guide students as they construct their products. One criterion on all rubrics is a category on interpretation of the basic principles.

Figure 3.14. **Gail's completed Multiple Menu Unit Plan for Section IV of the Knowledge Menu (back).**

4

The Instructional Techniques Menus

Effective teaching is not a set of generic practices, but instead is a set of context-driven decisions about teaching. Effective teachers do not use the same set of practices for every lesson. . . . Instead, what effective teachers do is constantly reflect about their work, observe whether students are learning or not, and, then adjust their practice accordingly.

—C. Glickman

Engaging students in the act of learning requires much consideration by the curriculum writer. Planning a unit involves a number of instructional decisions that are critical and must be made consciously and purposefully. Viewed broadly, the Instructional Techniques menus require educators to carefully consider how learning will take place as students interact with the content. The types of decisions that teachers make regarding which instructional techniques they will use to assist young people in the acquisition and application of knowledge become as important in the curriculum planning process as selecting the content for the instructional unit. The deeper the pool of strategies from which a teacher can select, the more variety he or she can offer students as they set about making meaning from these organized learning experiences.

The next set of menus (see Figure 4.1) from the model (Instructional Objectives and Student Activities Menu, Instructional Strategies Menu, Instructional Sequence Menu, Artistic Modification Menu, and the Instructional Products Menu) concern pedagogy, organization, and the sequence of lessons. Specifically, these menus provide curriculum developers with a range of options related to how they will engage students in the process of "uncovering" the

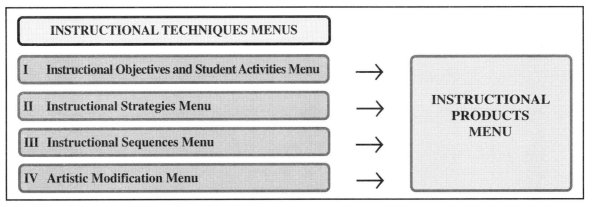

Figure 4.1. Instructional Techniques Menus.

authentic content of the Knowledge Menu.

The Instructional Objectives and Student Activities Menu

This combined menu of instructional objectives and student activities (Figure 4.2) is designed to provide the curriculum developer with a taxonomy of processes and behaviors that are used by learners as they construct knowledge about a discipline. This menu reminds the curriculum designer that in a well balanced curriculum activities must address both content and process objectives. The balance provides learners with practice in the spectrum of encoding and recoding activities associated with learning new information. By clarifying the process skills and sharing the objectives of the activities, students learn to identify and control their own thinking patterns and behaviors.

The first category of the menu (Assimilation and Retention) deals with information input or pickup processes. At this level, teachers need to decide how the students will acquire information about a particular event, topic, or concept: Will students take notes as they read a particular book? Will students need to make observations of a particular event and record the information on a chart? The second category (Information Analysis) focuses on a broad range of thinking skills that describe the ways in which information can be processed in order to achieve greater levels of understanding. At this level, teachers consider how their students will interact with the information: Will students be asked to compare and contrast pieces of information, tabulate data they have gathered, make predictions based on data they have collected, or summarize information? The third category (Information Synthesis and Application) deals with the output or products of the thinking process. At this level, teachers will make decisions to suggest avenues in which students can create new ways of using the information they have gathered or analyzed: Will students use the information to create a new model or explanation, produce a book, make a presentation, or develop a new theory? The final category (Evaluation) is also an output process, but in this case the focus is on the review and judgment of information in terms of aesthetic, ethical, and functional qualities. Teachers engaging students at this level might generate activities that help students judge the quality of a solution or determine whether something is worthy of receiving merit.

There are three important considerations the curriculum developer should keep in mind when using this menu. First, the four categories on this menu are not intended to be followed in a linear and sequential fashion. In the real world of thinking and problem solving, one must often cycle back to lower levels of information input and analysis activities in order to improve the scope and quality of the products and judgments. The overall process, therefore, must be viewed as a cyclical or spiraling sequence of interrelated activities rather than a linear chain of events.

The second consideration relates to the general goal of achieving both specificity and comprehensiveness in the overall process of curriculum development. Each unit and lesson should be developed in such a way that the curriculum writer is as certain about the process objective as he or she is about the content to be taught. Over a given period of time, the teacher should attempt to achieve comprehensiveness in process development by selecting a diverse range of objectives and student activities. In this regard, the curriculum developer should use this menu and the other instructional techniques menus as checklists that will help achieve balance as well as a catalog of processes from which selections can be made.

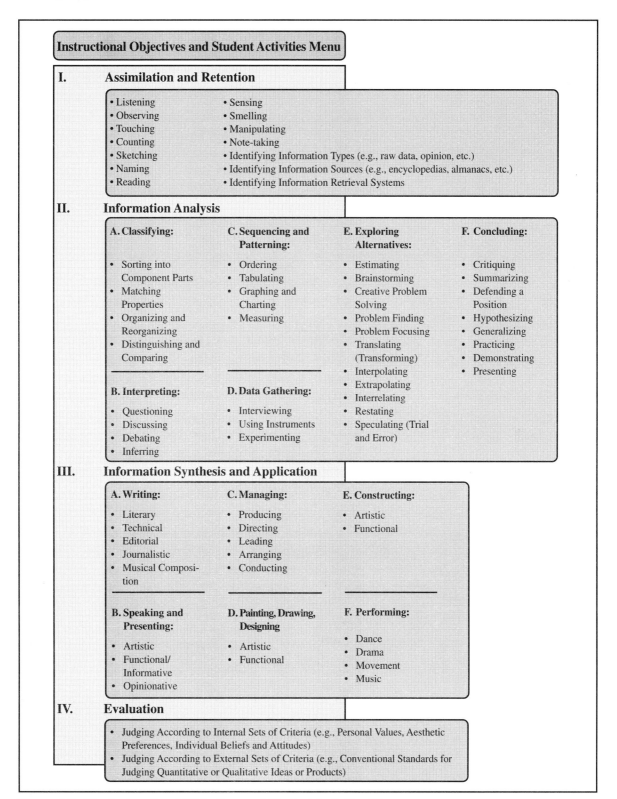

Figure 4.2. The Instructional Objectives and Student Activities Menu.

Finally, we have designed the objectives and activities in this menu to embrace the full range of affective processes. We have assumed that processes such as attending, receiving, and valuing take place in an integrated fashion when students pursue activities set forth in this menu and when such activities are combined with certain topics (knowledge) that enhance the development of affective processes. For this reason we did not include a separate affective menu in the model.

Gail's Journey:
Applying the Instructional Objectives and Student Activities Menu

In preparing her unit, Gail used this menu to consider what she would have the students do as they interacted with the content. First she generated a list of student activities and carefully considered how these activities would achieve her goal in helping the students uncover the meaning of the content she had selected for her unit. She asked herself questions such as "What types of activities would help the students gain information about archaeology?" "What types of activities will involve students in understanding what goes on at a dig site?" and "What types of process skills will I want the students to use in analyzing a civilization?" She then stated the answers to these questions in an instructional objective format. Listed below are several of her unit objectives:

Assimilation and Retention
- Students will *read and discuss* fiction and nonfiction selections about archaeology to *identify* how archaeologists define their field, how a culture is represented, and how archaeologists conduct their work.

- Students will *observe* archaeological digs and marine archaeology explorations on video to *discuss* how archaeologists use artifacts to understand a culture and to *identify* the tools and research procedures used by archaeologists.

- Students will *gather information* by using the "ask an expert" inquiry at the local field museum.

- Students will *participate* in a virtual dig on the World Wide Web

Information Analysis
- Students will *compare and contrast* various civilizations based on categories of information gathered in their research.

- Students will *demonstrate* how to measure, record, grid, and catalog artifacts at a historical site.

Synthesis and Application
- Students will *conduct* a dig at a historical site by applying the methodologies of the archaeologist.

- Students will *construct* a simulated dig for other students by applying what they have understood about a site.

Evaluation
- Students will *generate* a set of internal criteria to judge the quality and sustainability of a civilization they have researched.

Instructional Strategies Menu

The next menu, the Instructional Strategies Menu, provides a broad range of teaching strategies (e.g., discussion, dramatization, independent study) that represent the ways in which teachers organize learning situations. A variety of carefully selected instructional strategies from this menu provide students with multiple ways to be engaged with knowledge and to employ the full range of their intellectual abilities and learning styles. The strategies range from highly structured teaching methods to those in which greater degrees of self-directedness are placed upon the learner. Many of the strategies are used in combination with one another.

As is the case with menus discussed earlier, teachers should make an effort to achieve a balance in the use of these strategies. They should also work to develop curricular experiences for students that favor the less structured end of the instructional strategies continuum. This recommendation is consistent with the emphasis that educators place on both self-directed learning and creative productivity. Finally, teachers should attempt to match certain strategies with particular types of knowledge. Thus, for example, the simulation or role playing strategy might fit more appropriately with content dealing with a controversial issue, and the programmed instruction strategy would work well with content designed to teach computer operation skills.

Figure 4.3 lists various instructional strategies teachers use to engage young people in the act of learning. This list does not represent every instructional strategy, but it provides the curriculum writer with numerous options to consider when designing curricular activities.

Instructional Strategies Menu

- **Recitation and Drill**
- **Peer Tutoring/Teaching**
- **Programmed Instruction**
- **Lecture**
- **Discussion**
- **Guided or Unguided Independent Studies or Explorations**
- **Simulations**
- **Learning or Interest Center Activities**
- **Dramatization**
- **Role Playing**
- **Guided Fantasy**
- **Replicative Reports or Projects**
- **Investigative Reports or Projects**
- **Apprenticeships, Internship, and Mentorship**
- **Audiovisual Presentation**
- **Literature Circles**
- **Problem-based Learning**
- **Technology-supported Learning**
- **Grouping Strategies**
    Flexible Grouping
    Interest Grouping
    Skills Grouping
    Cooperative Learning
    Cluster Grouping
    Content Grouping
- **Storytelling**
- **Socratic Inquiry**
- **Advance Organizers**
- **Concept Mapping**
- **Oral Reading**
- **Interactive Video**
- **Shared Inquiries**
- **Experimentation**
- **Brainstorming**
- **Demonstration**
- **Field Trips**
- **Guest Speakers**
- **Group Debate**
- **Virtual Field Trips**
- **Internet/Computer Simulations**
- **"Ask an Expert" Inquiries**

Figure 4.3. The Instructional Strategies Menu.

Figure 4.4 takes some of the instructional strategies listed in Figure 4.3 and presents ways teachers can enhance these strategies to facilitate student learning.

Strategy Description	**Lecture** Oral presentation of information to small or large groups of students.

Enhancing the Strategy:

- Provide graphic organizers by having students identify key information which is then categorized in meaningful ways to assist learning the information. Information can be classified under a heading and related to the nucleus word or words that identify a primary topic. Vary the graphic organizers so that some of them reflect the sequence of events that need to be learned, causal relations that are explored, and interactions between problems and their solutions.
- Teach effective note-taking skills by dividing the note paper in half. On one side of the paper generate questions and on the other half provide the information to answer the questions.
- Provide handouts of information covered.
- Alternate between lecture and questions.
- Have students summarize information or react to the information after short periods of lecturing.
- Describe the topic in terms of its parallels to experiences and examples with which the students are likely to be familiar.
- Provide examples and nonexamples of the concepts being introduced (concept attainment strategy).
- Ask students to provide examples and nonexamples of the concepts being introduced (concept attainment strategy).
- Infuse storytelling into the lecture format.
- Invite guest speakers to address the class and share what they know about a topic.
- Use a variety of print and media resources to elaborate on or underscore a particular point.
- Include a demonstration or a presentation with slides.
- Assist students in forming concepts by asking open-ended questions designed to elicit as much data as possible from the class. Ask students to record the class' answers, organize the information into groups, and assign conceptual labels. For example, prior to a unit on democracy, a teacher might ask, "What do you think of when you hear the word democracy?" Students generate responses, organize the information into groups, and assign conceptual labels to explain the attributes of the groups (concept formation/diagnosis).
- Have students use manipulatives to facilitate an understanding of a concept.

Strategy Description	**Recitation and Drill** Instructional strategy used to help students learn information that can be retrieved efficiently.

Enhancing the Strategy:

- Teach specific strategies for recalling information (e.g., strategies for memorizing basic math facts, identifying principles that are shared by information being memorized, looking for relationships between the elements being learned, placing information within a contextual setting).
- Encourage students to categorize information based on attributes.
- Include game formats to strengthen student interest (*Jeopardy*, *What's My Rule*, *So You Want to Be a Millionaire*).
- Teach students to run their own practice sessions. Help them learn strategies for practicing their spelling words and then let the students practice with each other.

Figure 4.4. Enhancement strategies for instructional techniques.

Strategy	**Peer Tutoring and Teaching**
Description	Instructional strategy for pairing students in situations in which one person (tutor) who is knowledgable about a specific content area can assist another person (tutee) who does not fully understand or is not acquainted with the information, topic, or concepts.

Enhancing the Strategy:
- Pair students who share similar interests or in situations in which each person mutually benefits from the information shared.
- Have students become experts in particular topics so that they can share this information with other students who have selected other topics to pursue.

Strategy	**Discussion**
Description	Instructional strategy for promoting interaction between the teacher and the students or between groups of students.

Enhancing the Strategy:
- Vary the level of questions that are asked.
- Provide wait-time before a response is given and after a response is heard from the group.
- Listen to what students are trying to explain and follow up their questions with clarifying questions.
- Vary the strategies to engage students in discussion. Provide students with a set of questions that the class will explore and give them time to prepare their responses individually or in small groups.
- Allow students to generate their own questions about a topic or concept and encourage them to ask questions of each other. For example, let students organize their own discussion groups and require them to ask questions of each other.
- In reading, place students in literary discussion groups and allow them to generate a series of questions to ask each other about the book that they have read. Teach students to generate interpretive and evaluative questions.

Strategy	**Programmed Instruction**
Description	Self-teaching method in which material to be learned is arranged in a sequence of steps so that individual learners can work at their own speed.

Enhancing the Strategy:
- Use contracts to provide some students with opportunities to learn material that is more commensurate with their learning rate. The contract should outline what the student is to do, which resources the student should use, what kind of learning product the student should produce, which procedures will be used for evaluation, and a timeline for completing the project.
- On the Internet, create a "Webquest" and structure it so that students can work through a concept at their own particular pace.
- Use tutorials as a form of programmed instruction. (Many software programs include tutorials.)
- Realize that some students may need more guidance and support than others.

Strategy	**Problem-based Learning**
Description	Instructional strategy for organizing portions of the curriculum around ill-structured problems. Students simultaneously acquire new knowledge and experience in solving problems.

Enhancing the Strategy:
- Assist students in identifying problems and formulating research plans.
- Help students identify what they know and don't know about a problem.
- Provide resources which may assist students in their problem-solving.
- Provide methodological support to assist students in gathering and analyzing information (how to conduct interviews, how to design a survey, how to detect bias in historical accounts, etc.).

Figure 4.4. Enhancement strategies for instructional techniques (cont.).

Strategy Description	**Role Playing** Instructional strategy used to help students appreciate the perspectives of others, recognize the impact of decisions on others, or acquire an understanding for specific content by replicating the roles of people who participated in a real event.

Enhancing the Strategy:
- Design a problem or situation that is useful for exploring a particular concept. Design background information or have students investigate the background information that will assist them in carrying out their roles.
- Engage students in debates that have them explore opposing viewpoints.
- Have students play a role on a panel or forum to explore an idea or concept.
- Provide opportunities for students to dramatize an event. (Teachers have used this technique in science classes to assist students in understanding the function of various parts of a plant, organ, solar system, etc.)

Strategy Description	**Simulations** Instructional strategy used to place students in situations that closely parallel those found in the real world. Simulations simplify reality to highlight certain key ideas.

Enhancing the Strategy:
- Require students to assume roles, make decisions, and face the consequences of their actions.
- Provide time to introduce students to the simulation and time to explore their assigned roles and plot strategies.
- Play an active role in facilitating the process and debriefing the simulation through discussion.

Strategy Description	**Guided or Unguided Independent Studies or Explorations** Instructional strategy used to encourage individuals or small groups of students to pursue topics, real problems, controversies, or interests of their choice. Teachers or other adults facilitate students' work, which results in some type of product or service. The level of teacher involvement depends on students' prior experiences.

Enhancing the Strategy:
- Assist students in pursuing real problems that have the following characteristics:
  1. Students have an emotional or internal commitment in addition to a cognitive or scholarly interest in pursuing the problem.
  2. The real problem does not have existing or unique solutions. (This characteristic differentiates the problem from an exercise.)
  3. Students want to bring about some form of change in actions, attitudes, or beliefs on the parts of a targeted audience, or they want to contribute something new (to the students) to the sciences, arts, or humanities.
  4. The product or service is directed toward a specific, authentic audience (e.g., local historical society).
- Introduce students to various methodological and domain-specific skills to explore topics as practicing professionals would study them.
- Arrange for students to meet with individuals/mentors who might assist them in acquiring information.

Figure 4.4. **Enhancement strategies for instructional techniques (cont.).**

Gail's Journey:
Selecting the Instructional Strategies for the Archaeology Unit

Gail selected a variety of instructional strategies to facilitate the learning process for the students in her classroom. To provide an overview of the field of archaeology, she located an archaeologist and visited with him about what he might offer to the students. Gail knew that she wanted him to explain his work, how he studied his field, and the tools that he used to conduct his investigations. Her decision to invite the archaeologist into the classroom provided an authentic way to acquaint her students with archaeology. By having them generate a series of interview questions to ask the archaeologist, Gail encouraged her students to take an active role in acquiring information that would assist them in understanding how an archaeologist thinks and conducts his or her work.

Gail used the strategy of concept formation in many of her lessons by asking the students to generate a list of artifacts that a civilization leaves behind to reflect its history. Gail had the students take this list, categorize the information according to various attributes, and then assign a conceptual label to the information. In using this particular teaching strategy, Gail assisted students in formulating concepts from what they knew about their own culture. She used this technique to help the students obtain an understanding that the concept of artifact includes physical and documentary evidence and that artifacts reveal stories which help to explain a culture's recreational and social activities, modes of transportation, social status, etc.

In her planning, she also considered ways to engage students in pursuing the answers to their own questions. By learning how to facilitate individual or small group investigations, Gail built into her unit opportunities for students to self-direct the learning process: she had them gather data to compare various civilizations and encouraged them to pursue areas of study which were of personal interest.

Instructional Sequences Menu

The Instructional Sequences Menu (Figure 4.5) is based on the work of major learning theorists such as Gagné and Briggs (1979) and Ausubel (1968). Ausubel places considerable stress on meaningful learning, which involves relating the content of the lesson to the student's knowledge base, experiential background, and capacity to learn. He believes that "the most important single factor influencing learning is what the learner already knows. Ascertain this and teach him accordingly" (Ausubel, Novak & Hanesian, 1978). The specific aspects of their work that are reflected in this menu deal with the organization and sequence of events that help maximize the outcomes of a preplanned learning activity. This menu differs from the others in that the items are likely to be followed in a sequential fashion. It is important to point out that, since the menu is intended to be a helpful framework rather than a rigid prescription, the sequence may be "recycled" several times in a single unit or even a given lesson.

According to Gagné and Briggs (1979), an important consideration in sequencing instruction is to organize material in such a way that the learner has mastered necessary prerequisites. Prerequisites are broadly interpreted to include a favorable attitude toward the material to be learned as well as

Instructional Sequences Menu

I.   Gain Attention, Develop Interest and Motivation

- Tell a story about an event that is related to the lesson.
- Read a story that is related to the information.
- Begin a lesson with a discrepant event—and event that is contrary to what one might expect.
- Provide a brief demonstration that generates interest.
- Ask students to brainstorm what they already know about a concept and to share their thoughts.

II.   Inform Students about the Purpose/Objective of a Lesson or Lesson Segment and Provide Advance Organizers

- Provide a graphic or narrative organizer that will assist students in organizing ideas. For example, Gail started her unit by explaining to her students that humanity leaves evidence of their common culture in their artifacts. She then continued by stating to the students, "As you watch this video, I want you to identify the types of artifacts archeologists have located to help them understand this particular culture." By using an advance organizer, Gail has provided her students with a way to structure the ideas and facts in this learning experience.
- Use the principles and concepts of a discipline as advance organizers and then relate the lessons back to these ideas.
- Relate how the purpose of the lesson will help students accomplish a specific goal or answer a particular set of questions.
- Help students connect the objective of the lesson to other disciplines or with real life.

III. Relate Topic to Relevant Previously Learned Material

- Ask students to recall what they have already learned and address how this new information relates to their prior learning experience. "Do you remember yesterday when . . ."
- As students are in the process of learning something new, have them explain their strategies to their peers or have them explain how they arrived at a particular understanding. Have students talk out loud about what they have learned and how it is related to previous learning.

IV.   Present Material Through a Combination of Instructional Strategies and Student Activities

- Choose a variety of instructional strategies and design student activities that will engage students in the act of learning.
- Focus on strategies that will require students to interact with the content (e.g., look for examples or evidence, apply a concept to related disciplines or experiences, arrive at a solution to a problem, etc.)
- Monitor and coach students as they perform a task. Escalate student thinking as they work individually or in small groups.

V.   Provide Options/Suggestions for Advanced Level Follow-Up Activities on an Individual or Group Basis

- Listen carefully to student-generated questions and record these questions on a chart for future investigations.
- Generate a list of interesting projects related to the topic that may appeal to students.
- Ask students to consider what they don't know about a topic studied, but would like to know.
- Pose ill-structured problems that are relevant to students' lives and related to the topic or subtopic.

VI.   Assess Performance and Provide Feedback

- Embed assessment strategies throughout lessons:
  - Oral assessments
  - Essay assessments
  - Attitudinal assessment
  - Portfolio assessment
  - Anecdotal assessment
  - Performance-based assessment (specific tasks, presentations, product)
  - Student self-evaluation
  - Metacognitive coaching
  - Student observation/interview
  - Journaling
  - Debriefing/Questioning
  - Checklists

VII. Provide Advance Organizers for Related Future Topics

- Explain how concepts and principles are related to other disciplines. For example, how are the concepts of homeostasis in biology similar to or different from the concepts of disequilibrium, assimilation, or accommodation in a culture?

VIII. Point Out Transfer Opportunities and Potential Applications

- Arrange for students to take information they know and apply it to novel problems or a related topic.

Figure 4.5. Instructional Sequences Menu.

essential terminology, functional concepts, and basic factual information. It is for this reason that the Instructional Sequence Menu begins with an item that highlights the need for gaining attention and developing motivation. Gagné and Briggs also emphasize the value of relating present topics to relevant previously learned material and, whenever possible, integrating present topics into a larger framework that will add greater meaning to the topic at hand. This concern is dealt with, in part, through the strategies recommended in the first section of the Knowledge Menu, Locating the Discipline. Finally, Gagné and Briggs recommend that transfer not be left to chance; instead curriculum developers provide links between information learned and other situations in which such information may be applied. In a similar fashion, Ausubel's (1968) theory of meaningful learning maintains that learning is enhanced when students are provided with a preview or overview of the material to be taught and the ways in which the material is organized. These "advance organizers" can be most easily dealt with by making students aware of content and process objectives at the beginning of an instructional sequence and by connecting specific information back to the concepts and principles selected as the organizing frameworks for the unit.

The Artistic Modification Menu

Most teachers have had, at one time or another, the experience of teaching a lesson that was so successful and satisfying that at its conclusion they might have signed it (figuratively speaking) in much the same way that an artist signs a painting. This kind of personal involvement and excitement is more likely to occur when teachers use materials that they have developed themselves or in which they have a special personal interest. When teachers routinely use material prepared by others, some of the excitement and effervescence of good teaching is likely to be lost. Teachers can take steps to recapture the potential for excitement inherent in almost any curricular topic by applying a concept called artistic modification. This concept is an *invitation* to teachers to inject something of their own choosing and of personal relevance into curricular material that has been prepared by others.

Rationale and Description

A major part of the rationale underlying the concept of artistic modification is derived from the work of Philip Phenix (1987). He points out that instructional material can be either alive or dead, depending on the way it is used or misused in the teaching-learning process. According to Phenix, material is most appropriately used when it serves as an instrument for dialogue and active engagement. When material is imported from sources other than the teacher's own experience, it may assume an alien quality when not mediated by the teacher. Phenix points out that prepared curricular material is misused when taken literally and uncritically and when it is considered in only a theoretical and abstract context without constant concern for concrete application and practical outcomes.

Texts and other prepared curricular materials may not encourage the type of engagement and dialogue discussed above because they are often viewed as objective and authoritative presentations of information and reality. Such a view often discourages teachers from "tampering" with textbook content, thus minimizing opportunities for the kinds of dialogue that will make material personally meaningful for students. Phenix (1987) believes that if teachers are to make significant changes in student attitudes and conduct, they must reexamine the ways in which they adapt curricular material. Teachers can properly adapt materials by personalizing, interpreting, criticizing, and dissecting curricular material in ways that bring life and meaning to content. The problem, of course, is how teachers go about doing this type of adaptation. In those cases where teachers' guides are overly prescriptive, curriculum developers do not view adaptation as a legitimate part of teachers' roles. In addition, many teachers simply lack training and practice in bringing their own modifications to the curricular material they are using. The concept is also difficult to convey to teachers because the overuse of prescribed material prepared by others frequently results in an attitude that curricular content can come only from the "content experts." Such an attitude may cause some teachers to perceive themselves as not having the content background necessary to add material of their own to already prepared curriculum. Contrary to this perception, artistic modification does not require an extremely high level of content expertise because it is essentially a personalization process. Each teacher is the best expert of his or her own experience, and artistic modification is simply a process of inviting teachers to put this personalized experience into the material they are using.

In using the Artistic Modification Menu, teachers make their own creative contributions to previously developed materials. These modifications include criticizing and interpreting curricular content, examining content in relation to the teacher's own values and experiences, and adding content of the teacher's own choosing, even if additional material is in conflict with the prescribed content of a particular unit of study. Figure 4.6 presents eight categories and examples.

From a practical standpoint, we designed these categories and examples to help teachers analyze and understand the different ways in which artistic modifications can be made. Suggestions for modifications can be both general and specific, but they must always be personal rather than prescribed by textbooks or curriculum guides. The goal of this process is to encourage teachers to put themselves into the curriculum rather than drawing totally on the knowledge and experience of the person(s) who developed the material. A related goal is to create excitement and involvement within teachers so that they can, in turn, arouse interest, curiosity, and motivation on the parts of their students.

Designing Artistic Modifications

The Artistic Modification Template (Figure 4.7) is one strategy for generating artistic modification topics. The template is divided into three types of personal experiences: Direct, Indirect (or Vicarious), and Creative. Each type is further subdivided into categories that represent logical components of the three general types of experiences. Figure 4.8 is a completed example based on one teacher's experiences teaching World War II. Any one or a combination of these experiences can be integrated into standard curricular material on World War II and can serve as a starting point for developing an artistic modification experience or activity. Many items are the basis for "a story" about experiences that would not be included in textbook material. Most importantly, generating a list of artistic modification topics based on personal interest and enthusiasm for these topics and events helped this teacher energize both himself and his students about this period in history.

Teachers can also begin generating topics for artistic modification by working with others in a small group brainstorming situation. Group interaction often prompts a related idea that may evolve into a good teaching idea/activity. However, in order for a subsequent idea or activity to qualify as a personal artistic modification, it must be something that is relevant to the teacher and a product of his or her own experience. It is also a good idea for teachers to pursue this activity individually as a new unit of study or topic is being developed. Artistic modification should always be approached experimentally—that is, teachers should try various approaches with groups of students, and modify them according to students' reactions.

Reflecting upon material before teaching it, even if it has

Artistic Modification Menu

I. Share with students a personal experience that is directly or indirectly related to the content. (During a unit on Shakespeare, show personal slides of the rebuilt Globe Theater, Stratford-on-Avon, Anne Hathaway's cottage, and other sites related to the Elizabethan era.)

II. Share personal knowledge or insider information about a person, place, event, or topic. (While pursuing a unit on anthropology, point out a *Time* or *Newsweek* magazine article on the controversy surrounding the authenticity of Margaret Mead's research, or draw attention to biases reflected in news reporting about events in science or history.)

III. Share personal interests, hobbies, independent research, or significant involvements in personal activities. (Show students a family tree and/or immigration documents and share interesting family stories and archives while studying genealogy.)

IV. Share personal values, beliefs, and reflective experiences. (While working on a unit on American history, describe events related to personal participation in a civil rights demonstration, women's equality activities, or positions related to events or critical historical issues.)

V. Share personal collections, family documents, or memorabilia. (While studying the Civil War and the assassination of Abraham Lincoln, bring to class a collection of newspapers, magazines, etc. that describe the events surrounding the death of John F. Kennedy.)

VI. Interpret and share personal enthusiasm about a book, film, television program, or artistic performance. (Tell a "spy story" from a book such as *The Man Called Intrepid* while covering a unit on World War II.)

VII. Point out controversies, biases, or restrictions that might be placed on books, newspapers, or other sources of information. (Point out that magazines that depend heavily on advertising by tobacco and liquor corporations might tend to avoid publishing articles on the dangers of tobacco and alcohol.)

VIII. Other . . . There is no limit to the variety of personal touches that can make learning more engaging and relevant to students.

Figure 4.6. Artistic Modification Menu.

Multiple Menu Model

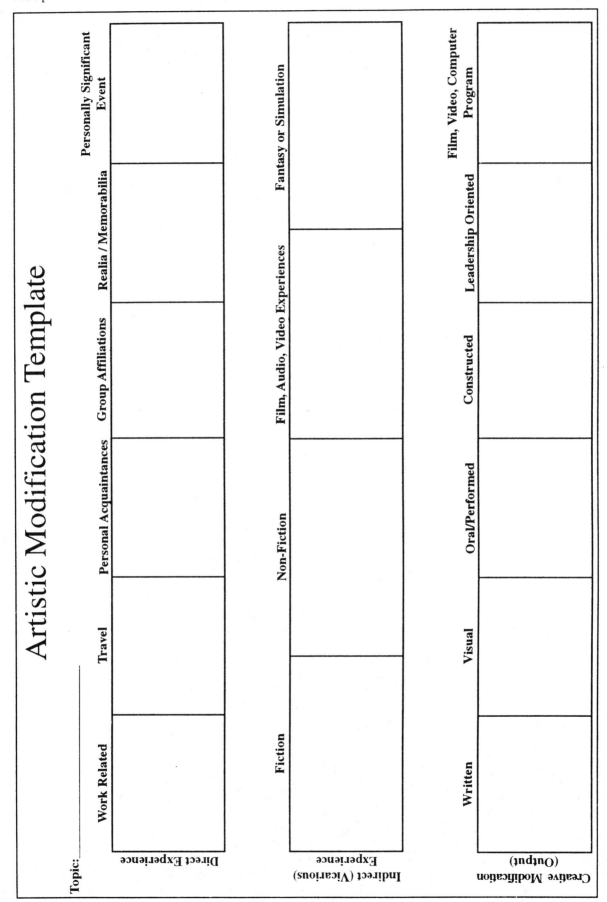

Figure 4.7. Artistic Modification Template.

Artistic Modification Template

Topic: World War II

Direct Experience

Work Related	Travel	Personal Acquaintances	Group Affiliations	Realia / Memorabilia	Personally Significant Event
• Mrs. Hutchinson's Victory Garden. • My midnight vegetable business	Visited WWII battle-fields in Europe and the Philippines (I have several brochures). Very touching experience.	• Hal Fisher (Pacific), • Peter Fedor (Whermacht), • Joe Marcotte (Bridge at Ramagan), • Josie Cavalier (Homefront 5 star mother)		• WWII souvenirs, • My own collection of spy/intelligence books • plane spotters manual	• watching sub patrols on NJ beach • blackouts and bomb sand • VE and VJ days

Indirect (Vicarious) Experience

Fiction	Non-Fiction	Film, Audio, Video Experiences	Fantasy or Simulation
Dozens--------Favorites • _The Naked and the Dead_ • _The Eagle Has Landed_	• _A Bridge Too Far_ • _Spies and Traitors of WWII_ Dozens of others . . . (see also info under Travel)	• "The Winds of War" • "War and Remembrance" Many others	There are some excellent simulations of famous WWII battles.

Creative Modification (Output)

Written	Visual	Oral/Performed	Constructed	Leadership Oriented	Film, Video, Computer Program
In high school I wrote and had published a short story about five survivors of a WWII battle.			As youngsters we were always build-ing models of WWII planes.		

Figure 4.8. Completed Artistic Modification Template.

been taught many times before, is as important to the teaching process as warm-up activities are for creating physical readiness and a positive mental attitude for the athlete. The interaction between prepared curricular material and the personal involvement of teachers will result in a "spontaneous combustion" that helps bring the material to life. In some cases, teachers may already be prepared to inject their own personal involvement into prepared material, but others may need to do some background reading or other types of preparation. Supplementary books on a particular topic may contain unusual insights, controversies, little known facts, or insiders' information usually not included in the regular material prepared for students.

Gail's Artistic Modifications and Other Examples

Gail used the art of personal stories and realia to provide examples of concepts and to bring life to the instructional material she prepared for her students. Her storytelling aroused interest, curiosity, and motivation on the part of her students. She told some stories to model how her students could draw from their experiences in a similar fashion.

The following anecdote is a detailed example of an artistic modification that Sally Dobyns, Associate Professor at the University of Southwestern Louisiana shared with her students. The story was used prior to introducing a lesson on using primary sources in historical research and illustrates the power of using personally relevant stories created by the teacher to introduce new concepts to her students.

"Sally Anne"

My first history lessons were family stories. My mother told mostly stories about her little sister, Sally. Born in 1934 when my mother was seven, Sally was the youngest of four children. She had the face of an angel, was full of mischief, and always played tricks on her older brother and sisters. She loved to play in water, any water. My grandparents put a lock on the kitchen door after Sally was discovered playing in the dog's water bowl. Not long after that, an outside lock also was put on the bathroom door.

Sally's favorite color was blue, she was afraid of the dark, and her favorite song was "I See the Moon." She learned to sing it when she was two years old, and she sang it over and over again to anyone who would listen. She "never met a stranger," loved everyone, and when the family went to town, she loved to chat with people in the stores. My grandmother fretted half-seriously that one day Sally might just walk off and go home with anyone who would listen to her little-girl tales and songs.

Sally was the light of my mother's life. My mom was Sally's "little mother," caring for her and teaching her as big sisters sometimes do. I have an old album, covered in soft, red suede that is filled with photographs of my grandmother and her four children. In every photograph, my mother is either touching Sally's shoulder or holding Sally's tiny hand in her own small one.

When Sally was five years old, she developed a strep infection. Penicillin was the treatment of choice, even in 1939, but there didn't seem to be enough of it to help Sally. My grandparents tried everything possible, seeking the finest medical treatment available. However, the infection began affecting Sally's heart, and it was at the Mayo Clinic in Rochester, Minnesota, in St. Mary's Hospital that Sally died.

Twelve years later I was born—the first granddaughter—so my mother gave me Sally's name. She also taught me all the ways in which Sally was special. She was part of me just as my parents, my sister and brother, and my grandparents were part of me. I felt close to a little girl I never met. At night, when my mother and I would look up at the sky, she would remind me to find the brightest star, the "window to heaven" from which Sally watched over me. The idea of stars being windows for guardian angels seemed perfectly logical to my young mind, and I had no doubt that I was watched over with care. I could feel it. Now I am grown, with nearly-grown children of my own, and I have learned the scientific definition of stars. Yet each time I look at the night sky, my eyes find the brightest stars, and for a moment, I wonder. When people who knew Sally described her as having the face of an angel, I knew this was true.

My image of Sally was not created from stories alone. For as long as I can remember there has been a portrait of Sally looking out from above my mother's piano. In July of 1948, my grandmother drove from Oklahoma City to Little Rock to meet with portrait artist Adrian Brewer. She took with her every photograph she had of Sally and shared with him stories of her little girl. The resulting portrait is splendid. In December of 1948, the portrait was over Mom's piano. And as long as her parents were living, my mother left the piano and portrait in their home where they belonged. The piano and portrait then spent some years in my mother's home; now the piano is in my home, and the portrait hangs over it. I have all the original photographs, and I've heard all the stories, so I know the portrait captures Sally's sweetness and intelligence perfectly—a blonde-haired, blue-eyed little girl sitting in a field of daisies—and in her eyes is the very beginning of a smile.

My mother and her mother were selective "packrats"; they never threw away anything that was "family-related." After my grandparents died, my mother brought several large boxes from their home to hers, each one a jumble of papers, pictures, diaries, and letters. Those boxes sat untouched in my mother's house for fourteen years; I didn't even know they existed. I found them after she too passed away, and I carried them to my home in Connecticut, where I began sorting through them. To the outside observer, these looked like ordinary old cardboard boxes filled with junk, but that was just camouflage for the treasures they held. In one of them, I found Adrian Brewer's original handwritten order for the portrait, "Sally Anne," with a price of $750. Also in that box was a typewritten letter from the artist to my grandmother telling her of the portrait's completion and that she could come to Little Rock to pick it up. The letter stated that he considered it his best work. I found diaries kept by my mother at ages 11 and 12 and by my grandmother during 1937. One day, I found paper cutout snowflakes crafted by Sally's five-year-old hands and a piece of shirt-cardboard on which she had tried to write the alphabet. These were in a sealed envelope upon which my grandmother had written that Sally had made them during her final stay at Mayo Clinic, almost exactly fifty years before I found them. On that day, as I unfolded one of the fragile snowflakes, those years fell away, and for a moment I touched Sally's hands.

When I tell this story, it seems at first to be a sad one. And yes, telling the story is difficult because it comes from a place deep inside me. Each time I must reach deep and find it and be reminded that almost everyone involved is now gone. But the very fact that I even have the pieces to the puzzle of a child I never met makes this quite a happy story, and in telling it I am able to thank those who gave it to me and to pass it on to my children who know all the players by heart. I tell it because I think it is important for students to learn about the family members who came before them and to take part in gathering this information and interpreting its relevance. Such self-knowledge is vital. It provides not only a sense of why we are who we are, but also a sense of where we fit in the scheme of things. For me, the stories and portrait of Sally were important pieces of the puzzle, but really just the beginning of my connection to her. They provided a framework and in part, an awareness of the value of treasures I would later discover in cardboard chests.

It has been in examining those other pieces of evidence about my family that I have been able to construct a far more complete picture, one that goes beyond Sally herself.

I am able to look back with historical perspective at the nine years between her illness and the hanging of the portrait, "Sally Anne," and in doing so, I see images of my mother's family life. During those years, World War II was fought, and Sally's older brother, a paratrooper, was injured at the Battle of the Bulge. During that time, my mother finished high school, got her first job, started college, and met my father. In those years, $750 was a very large sum of money. I envision my grandparents carefully saving and patiently searching for the right portrait artist; my grandmother driving twice to Little Rock on narrow, winding roads not in the least like the highways we travel now. I see her sitting in an artist's studio, sharing and trusting her child's memory to a man she'd never met. In the diaries, I found chronicles of daily life before, during, and after Sally, and I see the responses of the family members to those events and to each other. Holding the snowflakes, I celebrate the selfless courage of my grandmother as a young mother, sitting by the bed of her sick child, cheerfully keeping her entertained with scissors, paper, and pencil. But mostly, I see the young woman who was my mother telling stories about one little girl to another little girl, and later storing large boxes filled with memories, that were perhaps too painful for her to revisit. In her love, wisdom and sense of family, she saved them for someone else's discovery.

Instructional Products Menu

The Instructional Products Menu deals with the outcomes of learning experiences that the teacher presents. Two kinds of outcomes are likely to emerge during the learning process and are directly planned: concrete products and abstract products. Concrete products are the physical constructions young people create as they investigate the representative topics and interact with the principles, concepts and methodology of the discipline. These physical constructions may include products such as essays, videos, dramatizations, and experiments. Abstract products include observed behaviors such as increased self-confidence and leadership characteristics in addition to less obvious but equally important products such as problem-solving strategies and appreciation of the structures and functions of knowledge. It is important to note that the two kinds of products are mutually reinforcing. As students produce new kinds of concrete products, they will also demonstrate new abstract products, such as methodological skills and self-assurance. Likewise, as self-confidence and leadership opportunities increase, it is likely that students will create additional physical products as well.

Curriculum writers can use the lists presented in Figures 4.9 and 4.10 to generate a variety of concrete and abstract products that will help the learner demonstrate the type of learning that has occurred.

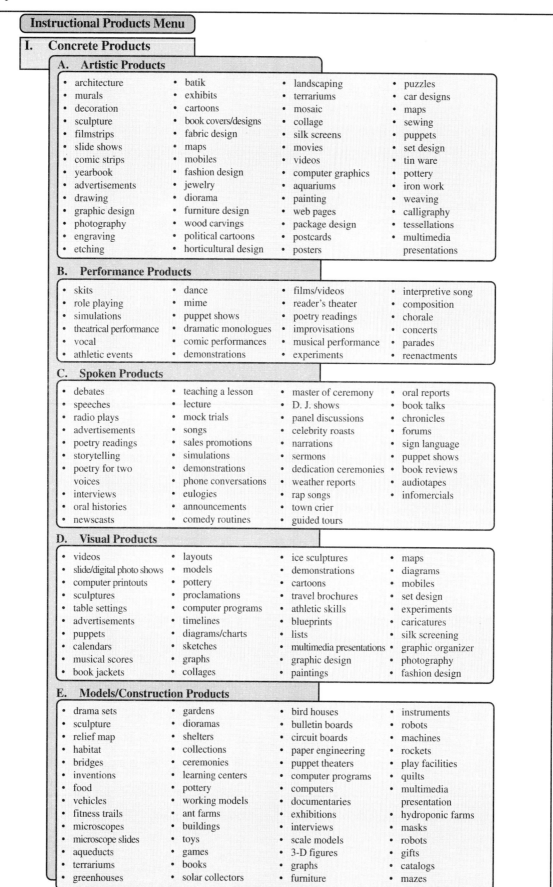

Instructional Products Menu

I. Concrete Products

A. Artistic Products

- architecture
- murals
- decoration
- sculpture
- filmstrips
- slide shows
- comic strips
- yearbook
- advertisements
- drawing
- graphic design
- photography
- engraving
- etching
- batik
- exhibits
- cartoons
- book covers/designs
- fabric design
- maps
- mobiles
- fashion design
- jewelry
- diorama
- furniture design
- wood carvings
- political cartoons
- horticultural design
- landscaping
- terrariums
- mosaic
- collage
- silk screens
- movies
- videos
- computer graphics
- aquariums
- painting
- web pages
- package design
- postcards
- posters
- puzzles
- car designs
- maps
- sewing
- puppets
- set design
- tin ware
- pottery
- iron work
- weaving
- calligraphy
- tessellations
- multimedia presentations

B. Performance Products

- skits
- role playing
- simulations
- theatrical performance
- vocal
- athletic events
- dance
- mime
- puppet shows
- dramatic monologues
- comic performances
- demonstrations
- films/videos
- reader's theater
- poetry readings
- improvisations
- musical performance
- experiments
- interpretive song
- composition
- chorale
- concerts
- parades
- reenactments

C. Spoken Products

- debates
- speeches
- radio plays
- advertisements
- poetry readings
- storytelling
- poetry for two voices
- interviews
- oral histories
- newscasts
- teaching a lesson
- lecture
- mock trials
- songs
- sales promotions
- simulations
- demonstrations
- phone conversations
- eulogies
- announcements
- comedy routines
- master of ceremony
- D. J. shows
- panel discussions
- celebrity roasts
- narrations
- sermons
- dedication ceremonies
- weather reports
- rap songs
- town crier
- guided tours
- oral reports
- book talks
- chronicles
- forums
- sign language
- puppet shows
- book reviews
- audiotapes
- infomercials

D. Visual Products

- videos
- slide/digital photo shows
- computer printouts
- sculptures
- table settings
- advertisements
- puppets
- calendars
- musical scores
- book jackets
- layouts
- models
- pottery
- proclamations
- computer programs
- timelines
- diagrams/charts
- sketches
- graphs
- collages
- ice sculptures
- demonstrations
- cartoons
- travel brochures
- athletic skills
- blueprints
- lists
- multimedia presentations
- graphic design
- paintings
- maps
- diagrams
- mobiles
- set design
- experiments
- caricatures
- silk screening
- graphic organizer
- photography
- fashion design

E. Models/Construction Products

- drama sets
- sculpture
- relief map
- habitat
- bridges
- inventions
- food
- vehicles
- fitness trails
- microscopes
- microscope slides
- aqueducts
- terrariums
- greenhouses
- gardens
- dioramas
- shelters
- collections
- ceremonies
- learning centers
- pottery
- working models
- ant farms
- buildings
- toys
- games
- books
- solar collectors
- bird houses
- bulletin boards
- circuit boards
- paper engineering
- puppet theaters
- computer programs
- computers
- documentaries
- exhibitions
- interviews
- scale models
- 3-D figures
- graphs
- furniture
- instruments
- robots
- machines
- rockets
- play facilities
- quilts
- multimedia presentation
- hydroponic farms
- masks
- robots
- gifts
- catalogs
- mazes

Figure 4.9. Instructional Products Menu: concrete products.

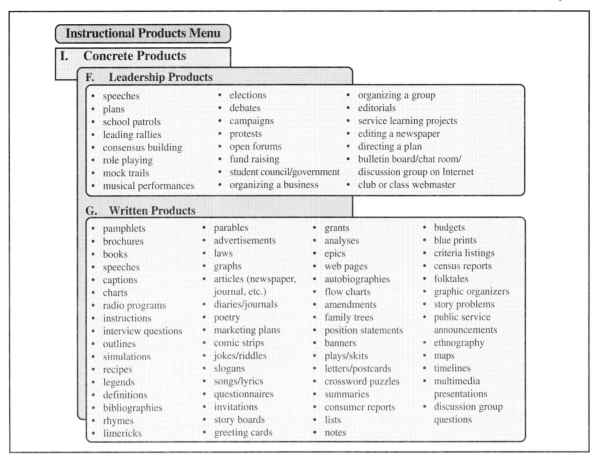

Figure 4.9. Instructional Products Menu: concrete products (cont.).

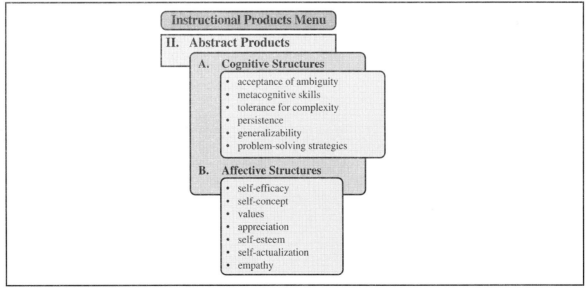

Figure 4.10. Instructional Products Menu: abstract products.

5

Curriculum By Design: Putting It All Together

Nothing happens unless first a dream.

—Carl Sandburg

The goal of the Multiple Menu Model is to achieve balance and coordination between knowledge and instructional techniques and to proceed from the abstract to the practical in the process of curriculum development. Writing curriculum is a complex task which defies simplification, but the curriculum writer can make the process more efficient by specifying the options that are available with regard to content and process and by pointing out procedures that can be used for blending together several factors that need to be considered simultaneously when developing curriculum.

Although we have presented several options that represent the structure of this model in the respective menus, two other conditions are necessary for the effective use of this model. First, the curriculum developer must understand the concepts presented on the menus. The appropriate use of an instructional activity such as extrapolating or an instructional strategy such as simulation will elude teachers if they do not have a practical understanding of both the concepts and how they can put them to work in a learning situation.

The second condition for successful use of this model involves some kind of plan or guide for synthesizing the respective menus at the practical or output level (i.e., actually writing curricular material). In developing this model, we have chosen to place knowledge at the center of the planning process and require curriculum designers to carefully consider what content and process understandings will become the focus of the instructional unit. To assist teachers in putting all the elements (menus) into operation, we have designed planning guides and templates for each section of the Knowledge Menu (see Appendices A and B). Teachers can use a set of forms called the *Lesson Planning Guides* to start gathering ideas. These four guides include suggestions and a series of questions for constructing the four sections of the Knowledge Menu. Each of the planning guides asks the designer to:

- Identify the location, definition, and organization of the field of study.
- Determine the principles and concepts that will be the central organizing framework of the unit.
- Select the methodologies that will be taught to the students to uncover the meaning behind the principles and concepts.
- Select representative topics that apply the basic principles, concepts and methodologies.

The structure of the *Lesson Planning Guides* encourages curriculum developers to consider each of the instructional techniques menus in conjunction with the preparation of content. Taken collectively, the menus and the planning guides direct curriculum developers to consider a broad range of options and to interrelate the many factors that must be considered when working to achieve balance and comprehensiveness in curriculum development.

The templates following the *Lesson Planning Guides* are graphic organizers or gathering tools for recording specific content and processes that the curriculum designer will consider using as he or she moves forward in creating student activities. The *Multiple Menu Unit Plan* (see Appendix B) is a template that teachers can use for storyboarding the lessons that they develop for each section of the Knowledge Menu. This form reminds the designer of the various menus to keep in mind when constructing learning activities. By reviewing choices over several different lessons or units of instruction, curriculum writers can determine whether or not they are giving equal consideration to the various categories of knowledge and the wide array of objectives, instructional strategies, and other techniques specified by the menus.

The *Artistic Modification Template* (see Appendix B) helps teachers generate ideas for artistic modifications that would be appropriate for the lessons being taught. Teachers should consider their best personal experiences with the content that they can share with their students.

What We Know From Teaching the Multiple Menu Model

Teachers who have used the Multiple Menu had previously concluded that curriculum was a set of activities handed to them that were designed to accomplish a particular objective deemed to be important by the district. As they moved forward in creating more authentic curricular units, they asked us many questions about how to use the Multiple Menu Model effectively. Listed below are our suggestions to teachers as they embark on this journey of curriculum writing.

1. What will the end product be?

The goal is to write a unit based on a field of study or discipline. The unit is divided into four sections, each based on the structure of knowledge. Within each section of the unit, there will be a set of learning activities that have been developed using the Instructional Techniques Menus. The purpose of these activities is to help the students understand how a discipline is organized, how its content is organized around principles and concepts, what methodologies are used by those who study this discipline, and to which areas or topics they can apply these concepts, principles, and methodologies. The Multiple Menu Model takes the teacher and students to the very heart of a discipline to examine its location in the domain of information and to understand the methodology employed by those who produce knowledge in the field. Accordingly, a teacher's instructional unit should enable learners to become firsthand inquirers and creators of information, a far more intensive, productive engagement in the school setting than what students experience as consumers of information.

2. What are fields of study?

The first task is for the teacher to choose a field of knowledge that is familiar and for which he or she has a passion. Designing curriculum can be tedious; therefore, the curriculum writer must be able to sustain an interest in the field he or she has selected. As with student research projects, high interest in the topic tends to motivate the curriculum developer to complete the task at hand. It has been our experience that the most successful units were written by teachers who put themselves "into" the writing process. They viewed this writing experience as an opportunity to be a creative producer. As they worked through the development of their units, their efforts went into understanding the model, its components, and the structure of the field of study they had chosen as their curricular focus.

We have also watched teachers struggle to find the field of study in which a certain topic is located. In some cases, a teacher may have to search for principles and concepts within a larger field of study. For example, for her archaeology unit, Gail located principles and concepts from the field of anthropology. Another example comes from a fourth grade teacher wanted to create a unit on *How Seeds Travel*. This was the title of a chapter in her science textbook that was introduced each year to the fourth grade students. To place this topic in a proper context and to assist students in seeing the "wholeness" of this idea, she began her search in the field of botany. She gathered reference materials to help her understand botany and found that one of the basic concepts in this field included the reproduction of plants. After researching the field of botany by reading articles, browsing through how-to books, and visiting with botanists, she felt that the textbook material was too simplistic and did not offer the depth she wanted to offer her students. In returning to the discipline, this teacher was able to place *How Seeds Travel* in a more proper and authentic context for her students as she designed learning experiences that required her students to assume the role of botanists.

In order to choose a field of study, we have found it helpful to understand the characteristics of a discipline. These characteristics help curriculum developers make sure that they place topics within their proper discipline.

For example, bubbleology is a fun way to involve students in the study of optics and surface tension, but it is the concepts and principles of physics that provide learners with the understanding of bubbleology. Nixon (1976) has created a list of characteristics which may assist the curriculum writer in determining whether selected fields of study can be justified (see Figure 5.1).

We have also found it helpful for teachers to begin looking at their current level of knowledge regarding various fields of knowledge. Often, because of the structure of textbooks, teachers lose sight of where the information or content they are presenting came from in the first place. In this process of teaching topics, they might not place knowledge in its proper context or help students develop systems of organization for the content and tools that they are acquiring. The "ologies and ographies chart" in Figure 5.2 is a gentle reminder of these fields of knowledge. Teachers should notice that on the right-hand side of this chart is a listing of the more typical topics educators might use as the focus of an instructional unit. We ask that teachers give proper consideration to organizing topics within their respective fields of study so that learners engage in a more authentic and accurate way of exploring the content.

3. How do I find the principles, concepts, and methodologies of the field?

- *Content Expert.* A curriculum developer who knows someone who will act as a content or knowledge consultant in a particular field of study will be able to verify the authenticity of the basic principles and functional concepts, methodologies, and representative topics of the discipline that the writer has identified. A friendly content area consultant can save the curriculum

---

Criteria of a Discipline

Identifiable Domain:	The persons working in a discipline or field of study must ask vital and important questions, deal with significant themes, maintain scope of inquiry, include a central core of interest, and have a beginning point and a set of goals.
History and Tradition:	An established history and tradition of scholarly pursuit must be a part of the field of study.
Structure:	The field of study should have a set of basic concepts. There should be a relationship between the concepts of the field and between the concepts and the facts of the discipline.
Integrity:	The discipline must have a wholeness, or undividedness, and a sense of completeness about it.
Procedures and Methods:	The discipline should use conceptual, technical, and mechanical tools to add knowledge to the field. It should follow a set of rules and a set of basic procedures that lead to ways of knowing and learning.
Process:	Process should be as much a part of the field of study as its products, knowledge, principles, and generalizations.
Accurate Language:	A precise and careful communication within its ranks and to outsiders should be a part of a discipline.

Figure 5.1. Criteria of a discipline.

Do You Know Your Ologies and Ographies?

1. Aerology .... **is** the study of .... the atmosphere in relation to flying. (x)
2. Anthropology .... is the study of .... human races. (oo)
3. Araenology .... is the study of .... spiders. (gg)
4. Archaeology .... is the study of .... the past through its materials and remains. (y)
5. Astronomy .... is the study of .... the stars. (pp)
6. Audiology .... is the study of .... the sense of hearing. (s)
7. Cardiology .... is the study of .... the heart. (uu)
8. Cartography .... is the study of .... mapping. (xx)
9. Cetology .... is the study of .... whales. (o)
10. Choreography .... is the study of .... dance. (l)
11. Chronology .... is the study of .... time sequence. (k)
12. Cinematography ...... is the study of .... motion picture photography. (e)
13. Cryptology .... is the study of .... deciphering codes. (ee)
14. Crystallography .... is the study of .... the classification of crystals. (aa)
15. Cytology .... is the study of .... cells. (ll)
16. Demography .... is the study of .... population, size, density, and distribution. (m)
17. Demonology .... is the study of .... evil spirits. (a)
18. Dermatology .... is the study of .... the skin. (v)
19. Ecology .... is the study of .... organisms and their environments. (qq)
20. Entomology .... is the study of .... insects. (ii)
21. Epidemiology .... is the study of .... contagious diseases. (f)
22. Epistemology .... is the study of .... knowledge. (w)
23. Ethnography .... is the study of .... descriptions of specific cultures. (d)
24. Etymology .... is the study of .... word origins. (i)
25. Gemology .... is the study of .... gems. (hh)
26. Genealogy .... is the study of .... ancestry. (jj)
27. Geography .... is the study of .... the earth's changing surface. (b)
28. Geology .... is the study of .... the earth's crust. (dd)
29. Gerontology .... is the study of .... aging. (c)
30. Graphology .... is the study of .... handwriting. (h)
31. Herpetology .... is the study of .... reptiles. (rr)
32. Histology .... is the study of .... living tissue. (q)
33. Holography .... is the study of .... laser light to produce images. (mm)
34. Hydrology .... is the study of .... water. (ww)
35. Ichthyology .... is the study of .... fish. (cc)
36. Laryngology .... is the study of .... the throat. (vv)
37. Lithography .... is the study of .... printing from a plane surface. (ff)
38. Meteorology .... is the study of .... weather and climate. (g)
39. Myrmecology .... is the study of .... ants. (nn)
40. Oceanography .... is the study of .... ocean environments. (tt)
41. Ontology .... is the study of .... existence, being. (n)
42. Ornithology .... is the study of .... birds. (j)
43. Osteology .... is the study of .... bones. (t)
44. Otology .... is the study of .... the ear. (u)
45. Paleography .... is the study of .... ancient writing. (z)
46. Paleontology .... is the study of .... fossils. (bb)
47. Penology .... is the study of .... prison and punishment. (kk)
48. Petrology .... is the study of .... rocks. (r)
49. Photography .... is the study of .... producing images with light. (p)
50. Psychology .... is the study of .... the mind, emotions, and behavior. (ss)

(Letters in parentheses correspond with quiz letters on page ii.)

Figure 5.2. Ologies and ographies.

developer much time and effort. In the same way, the content expert can save time and effort by using the expertise of an instructional expert.

Teachers can invite individuals who are currently practicing professionals in a specific field of knowledge to demonstrate to students how they conduct their research. These experts can teach a group of students how to use specific equipment to gather data when a teacher is not sure of the proper procedures or techniques. They can also serve as mentors to a group of students pursuing individual or group investigations. And, yes, they can become teachers' personal mentors as they become more knowledgeable about specific fields of study. For example, one teacher relied on an orthopedic surgeon in her community to teach her how to introduce Newton's Law to her fourth grade students. This surgeon enjoyed model rocketry and built rockets from scratch. Not only was he able to extend her knowledge of Newton's Laws, but he also happened to have the technological equipment and computer software to track the flight patterns of rockets. He offered to work with the class on Wednesdays to design rockets with tracking devices that would test various scientific principles. Not only did the students learn from this individual, but the teacher increased her understanding by working with him as well. While it may not be possible to know all the methodologies, principles, and concepts to the level of expertise that the practicing professionals do, we do believe that teachers should actively search for individuals who can help their students in acquiring advanced levels of knowledge. It is often these content specialists who have access to the equipment and technology not available in schools and can introduce them to students. Teacher should ask these experts to help them create student learning opportunities that are more authentic and respectful of the content and processes they are trying to teach.

- *Reference Librarian.* Another source of professional assistance is the reference librarian. These professionals are familiar with the structure of many disciplines and can help the curriculum writer locate reference books that will help construct meaningful and authentic curricular activities. Librarians can also assist the curriculum writer in obtaining materials that may be located at other universities or appeal to those experts that can be reached through electronic media.

- *Academic Standards.* Teachers can look to professional academic standards written by the various curriculum groups (e.g., National Council of Teachers of Mathematics, National Science Teachers Association, National Council for the Social Sciences, etc.) to identify the principles, concepts, methodologies, and representative topics within certain content areas. A curriculum designer will often have to reword these standards to reflect the principles and concepts in the fashion that we have suggested in Chapter 3. These resources typically list the methodologies to use, but they are not as specific as a how-to book would be on demonstrating skills and procedures. Consequently, we recommend that teachers search for lab manuals from college text books and specific "how-to" books that explain these methodologies in detail. How-to books are typically written to assist students in learning a skill or procedure important to the methodology of a field of study or a specific discipline. (Appendix D lists useful how-to resources).

- *Internet.* The World Wide Web is a very useful tool in locating information about specific areas of study. Teachers can search the databases, organizations, and speak to experts in almost every possible field of knowledge. It is not uncommon to find copies of historical documents or postings of important discoveries and interesting information about representative topics. For example, when searching for archaeological information, Gail located professional organizations that the students could write to for information, identified archaeologists who would serve as mentors to the students, explored archaeology websites that would help her students in gathering information about various civilizations, and obtained access to universities which specialized in archaeology.

- *Propedias.* We suggest using the macropedia and micropedia from the *Encyclopedia Britannica* to begin a search of various disciplines and to assist in creating a Knowledge Tree. Teachers can use macropedia (Knowledge in Depth) encyclopedias to help locate and identify the field of study within a discipline and how the discipline is organized. These encyclopedias provide an outline of the discipline that can serve to help the writer design a Knowledge Tree for students.

- *Journals in the Field.* Reference materials such as research articles, monographs, government documents, and magazines related to the discipline can also be helpful in acquiring information. By browsing through magazines such as *Dragonfly* (published in Scientific American Explorations), *Consumer Report, Science News,* and other content-specific magazines, teachers can locate interesting and often controversial issues to pursue within a particular field of study. Most fields of study have consumer-friendly magazines as well as professional research journals that communicate information about its field to other interested people. In some cases, publishers have developed magazines for children which try to accomplish a similar goal, but in a kid-like manner. *Dragonfly* is a magazine for young explorers that encourages students to submit for publication any research investigations they have conducted. Each issue is based on a theme and practicing professionals within various fields of study write about their work and the types of investigations they explore. One particular theme was *Investigating People and Plants*. The lead article was an interview written by a student about her father, an ethnobotanist. She described his work, the type of research he conducts, and stressed how his research is used by others. The magazine also includes investigation ideas posed by researchers to encourage students to participate in some global research study.

4. Are there other materials that are helpful to the curriculum writing process?

Curriculum writers should locate a copy of *Bloom's Taxonomy* (1954) to use as they design activities to help the students understand the four content areas.

5. How do I know if my lessons appeal to the imagination of students?

"Good teaching is imaginative in quality, and the effective teacher chooses materials that kindle the imagination of the learner " (Phenix, 1964, p. 342). In order to engage students' imaginations, teachers need to involve students in the process of exploring content in meaningful ways. When choosing instructional strategies, a teacher should consider questions such as "What types of activities will actively involve my students in uncovering these content ideas?" "What methodological skills can I teach that will actively engage students in constructing knowledge about a particular concept?" "What questions will I pose to the students to place them in direct confrontation with knowledge?" and "What issues are perplexing and relevant to them as we explore a concept?" When teachers design curriculum to address these questions, students should know the purpose behind what they are doing. They should feel like they have an important role to play in constructing some meaning behind these concepts or ideas.

The most brutal of all curriculum evaluators should be the students. If teachers are trying to develop curriculum activities that appeal to the imagination of young people, they must "try out" their units or activities on students, ask for their feed back, and then adjust accordingly to these recommendations.

6. Are there some organizational techniques that others have used to help them to accomplish this task?

In order to organize their curriculum writing experiences, some writers might find it helpful to establish folders for each section of the unit. They can use these folders to collect ideas and materials that they will use to develop the set of activities for each section of the unit. A separate folder for artistic modification ideas and teacher support materials can also be helpful. While this may appeal to those writers who are systematic, other curriculum writers may prefer a less structured filing approach to organizing their materials.

We have found that there are already published curricular materials that are authentic to specific disciplines and quite useful in helping students acquire content and process knowledge. When curriculum designers understand how knowledge is constructed, teachers can use these more appropriately with students to develop particular conceptual or methodological understandings.

7. I don't understand the importance of Artistic Modifications. Why should I use this menu?

Teachers should pay particular attention to the Artistic Modification Menu! It is the avenue through which their interest and the interests of their students can meet most frequently. Liberal use of Artistic Modification strategies engages learners and encourages them to pursue the area of knowledge selected. By injecting personal experiences and background into each unit, teachers and students can share interests, students learn to consider their own experiences, and they may develop a passion for the topic. Even though teachers can use various strategies from dramatic productions to sharing a favorite cartoon strip from childhood, it is important to remember that what makes artistic modification authentic is personal experience with the content.

8. Can I use the Multiple Menu Model with all types of learners?

Curriculum writers can use the Multiple Menu Model to develop differentiated curriculum for all types of learners. The model places a premium on the organization and pursuit of authentic knowledge; uses investigative methodologies; deals with complex structures, principles, concepts, and research methods; emphasizes higher level thinking skills, less structured teaching strategies, controversial issues, beliefs, and values; teaches concepts and principles as opposed to trendy topics and transitory information; focuses on representative topics which are used as a vehicle for process development; and emphasizes concrete and abstract products as oppose to factual assimilation. What the curriculum designer will need to consider is how he or she will differentiate the lessons to accommodate the vast array of student diversity within the classroom, making sure that respectful learning is arranged based on individual learning profiles (i.e., a student's strengths, content and skill level accomplishments, interests, and styles). We believe that the four areas of knowledge can vary in depth and complexity, concreteness and abstraction, depending on the questions a teacher asks, the examples which illustrate certain concepts and principles, the processes teachers select to engage the students, and the instructional materials that they place in the hands of young people. Teachers must be cognizant of making these ideas relevant to their students, and this goal requires that teachers know their students on a personal level.

Attributes of the Multiple Menu Model correspond with the guiding principles of curriculum differentiation for the gifted and talented (Passow, 1983). They place a premium on understanding the structure of a discipline, engaging students in methodological skills, and exposure to advanced content and concepts.

The Multiple Menu Model is also effective as a planning guide for non-school learning environments. We have watched teachers use this model to create opportunities for students to work with practicing professionals during Saturday programs and summer camps to learn principles and concepts of certain fields of study, engage students in applying the methodologies to short-term investigations, and explore related topics in-depth. Students select the field of study (e.g., botany, cinematography, architectural design, musicology, etc.) that they want to participate in for the week or two weeks of the camp and then work with other interested youth and their mentors to develop valuable products or services.

Appendix A

Lesson Planning Guides

Constructing the Knowledge Tree

Goal Statement:

To construct a graphic representation (Knowledge Tree) of a field of study that locates the selected field in the broad spectrum of knowledge and provides information about the relationships of the subdivisions within the field of study.

Materials Needed:

- College Textbooks
- Content Standards
- Macropedias
- Content Area Specialists
- Reference Books
- Card Catalog
- Micropedias

Steps:

I.   Research

1. Using the research materials listed above, start reading about your field of study so that you understand how it fits into the broad spectrum of learning. The questions you will be trying to answer include the following:
    - What subdivisions exist within this field of study?
    - How is this field of study related to other fields? and
    - How are the subdivisions within the field related to each other?

2. Using macropedias, micropedias, and the card catalogs in a library, examine how the selected field of study is organized and divided into subdivisions.

3. Examine textbooks and general and specific reference books to discover how the field of study has been represented by authors and researchers. (Many authors provide an overview of their field in introductory chapters.) In some reference books, authors have included knowledge trees to help define a particular field of study.

4. Talk to a reference librarian about how knowledge in general is organized and divided. Libraries are organized using a knowledge tree type of system.

5. Talk to an expert in your field of study and ask how he or she believes the field of study is organized. Ask for materials that deal with this issue as well as the names of "classic" textbooks

that examine the field of study in relationship to other branches of knowledge.

6. Visit a university bookstore and locate supplementary materials that accompany textbooks. Guidebooks, lab books, field guides, charts, handout packets, and monographs will add to your understanding of the field of study.

II. Generating Lists

After researching the field of study, the next step is to organize the information into several lists.

1. Create a list of the general divisions of knowledge (art, science, humanities, etc.)

2. A second list should include the fields of study within the general division that your field of study is located. For example, for a field of study located within the sciences, your list would include topics such as biology, chemistry, physics, etc.

3. The third list should include the subdivisions and topics that are found within your field of study.

III. Drafting a Knowledge Tree

1. Construct a rough draft of a graphic organizer, diagram, web, or "tree" that represents, illustrates, and organizes your field of study in the broad spectrum of knowledge in addition to the subdivisions within the field of study. Use the *Knowledge Tree Template* to design your graphic. Arrows, dotted lines, and other symbols can denote relationships that exist between and among the subdivisions.

2. Show the rough draft to a knowledge expert and an instructional expert. Ask for feedback on how well it represents and communicates the field of study and its subdivisions.

IV. Revision of the Knowledge Tree

1. Use the information received from the experts and the questions listed below to revise the Knowledge Tree graphic.

   • Is the Knowledge Tree logical?
      Does it start from the general fields and become more specific?
      Does it narrow the field of study to its subdivisions?
      Is it easy to follow and understand?

- Is the Knowledge Tree accurate?
    Do the connecting branches denote the correct relationship?
    Do the connecting branches flow in the correct direction?
    Are the subdivisions spaced and sized correctly?
- Is the Knowledge Tree clear?
    Can another person read and understand the field of study?
    Can you easily explain the Knowledge Tree to someone else?
- Does the Knowledge Tree teach?
    Does it locate the field of study?
    Does it organize the field of study?
    Will it attract and hold your students' attention?
- Is the Knowledge Tree artistically appealing?
    Is it spaced appropriately?
    Does it use meaningful symbols?
    Is it attractively arranged on the page?

V.   Second Draft of the Knowledge Tree

1. Construct a second draft of the Knowledge Tree on one sheet of paper.

2. Include a list of 3-5 key references that can be used for further study of the field.

VI.   Field Test the Knowledge Tree

1. Show the Knowledge Tree to friends, colleagues, experts, or practicing professions in the field of study and ask them for feedback.

2. Use the Knowledge Tree with a small group of students. Conduct orientation activities to acquaint the students to the field of study based on what is identified on the Knowledge Tree. Note the students' reactions and statements. Determine if the Knowledge Tree locates and organizes the field of study for the students. Make additional revisions based on the results of the field test.

Section I: Identifying the Location, Definition, and Organization of a Field of Knowledge

Goal Statement:

To locate, define, and organize a field of knowledge; provide an explanation of the general nature of the field; assist in understanding how a particular field of study fits into the "big picture" of knowledge; and explain the relationships of the subdivisions within a specified field of study.

Materials Needed:

- College Textbooks
- Knowledge Tree
- Reference Books
- Instructional Materials

Steps:

1. Considering the age and grade level of the students, the field of study, and the task of locating, organizing, and defining a field of study, select the questions that you will address in Section I of the unit. Use the *Gathering Information Template* to organize your information.

   - How is this field of study defined?
   - What is the overall purpose or mission of this field of study?
   - What are the major areas of concentration of each subdivision?
   - What kinds of questions are asked in each subdivision?
   - What are the major sources of data in each subdivision?
   - How is knowledge organized and classified in this field or subdivision?
   - What are the basic reference books in this field or subdivision?
   - What are the major professional journals?
   - What are the major databases? How can we gain access to them?
   - Is there a history or chronology of events that will lead to a better understanding of the field or subdivision?
   - Are there any major events, persons, places, or beliefs that are predominant concerns of the field, or best case examples of what the nature of the field of study is concerned with researching?
   - What are some examples of "insider's knowledge" such as field-specific humor, trivia, abbreviations, acronyms, "meccas," scandals, hidden realities, or unspoken truths.

2. Generate several introductory activities that assist students in locating, organizing, and defining the selected field of study.

Use the ***Multiple Menu Model Unit Plan Template*** to storyboard your ideas.

3. Use the Instructional Strategies Menu, the Instructional Objective/Activities Menu, the Instructional Sequence Menu, the Artistic Modification Menu, and the Instructional Products Menu to create a series of activities that address the questions you selected from the above list.

4. Check the activities for validity by answering the following questions and by asking a colleague or content area specialist to review these lessons.

   - Do the activities locate, organize and define the field of study?
   - Do the activities have variety, balance, and provide depth?
   - Do the lessons appeal to the imagination of students?

5. Using the Knowledge Tree and other assessment techniques, obtain feedback from the students and assess what they have learned about this field of study.

6. Find out if there is anything in students' daily lives, contemporary literature, music, television, or movies to which the topics and activities might relate.

7. Make modifications to the activities based on the validity check and the field test.

Section II: Identify the Basic Principles and Functional Concepts

Goal Statement:

To develop lessons that identify, instruct, and illustrate basic principles and functional concepts that are central to a field of study.

Materials Needed:

- College Textbooks
- How-To Books
- Content Specialists
- Lab Manuals
- Discipline-Specific Journals
- Researchers in the Field of Study

Steps:

1. Survey college texts and other reference books to generate a list of all the basic principles and functional concepts associated with the selected field of study. Instructor's manuals often offer information on basic principles and functional concepts. Turn these principles into generative questions that students can use as springboards for developing their own inquiries. Use the ***Principles, Concepts, and Student Inquiries Template*** to organize these thoughts.

2. Contact researchers or content area specialists to confirm or deny the authenticity of your list of basic principles and functional concepts. Tap into the resources that are available on the World Wide Web. Curricular organizations in a specific field of study can often provide valuable information to support your search.

3. Using the Instructional Objectives and Student Activities Menu, the Instructional Strategies Menu, the Instructional Sequence Menu, the Artistic Modification Menu, and the Instructional Products Menu, develop student activities and lessons that introduce the basic principles and functional concepts that you have selected for this unit. Use the ***Multiple Menu Model Unit Plan Template*** to begin storyboarding your ideas.

4. Check the validity of the lessons:

   - Determine if there is a logical sequence in which the basic principles and functional concepts should be taught.

   - Ask a content area specialist, a researcher in the field of study, or a colleague to review the sequence in which you plan to teach the basic principles and functional concepts.

- Check the lessons for balance, variety, sequence, and authentic use of vocabulary from the field of study.

- Field test the activities with students to check for interest. Determine if the activities or lessons relate to the students' lives in a meaningful manner.

- Review the lessons to ascertain if graphics, visuals, or technology-supported software and equipment will make the lessons more authentic.

Section III: Identifying the Methodologies

Goal Statement:

To develop lessons that identify, instruct, and apply investigative procedures that are followed in a selected field of study.

Materials Needed:

- College Textbooks
- How-To Books
- Lab Manuals
- Discipline-Specific Journals

Steps:

1. Considering the age and ability of the students, the nature of the field of study, and the skills that need to be taught, list the methodological skills and processes (general and specific) that are used by the practicing professions in the field.

2. Using the generated list, select the methodologies that are essential to the field of study and can be successfully taught to the age and grade level of the students with whom you are working. Place the methodologies in a logical or natural sequence. Use the ***Methodologies Template*** to organize your ideas.

3. Develop the student activities and lessons using the Instructional Objectives and Student Activities Menu, the Instructional Strategies Menu, the Instructional Sequence Menu, the Artistic Modification Menu, and the Instructional Products Menu to develop lessons which apply the research methodologies of the field of study. Keep in mind that the lessons must include activities that require students to actually practice using the methodologies. For example, if you were teaching students about how sociologists gather data through interviews, you should give students the opportunity to conduct interviews to understand how researchers conduct research or produce new knowledge. "How-to" books within a field of study can play a crucial role in providing students with the necessary skills to understand the "modus operandi" of the practicing professional. If a how-to book is difficult to find, call a practicing professional! Use the ***Multiple Menu Model Unit Plan Template*** to storyboard your lesson ideas.

4. Check the validity of the lessons:

   - Ask a content area specialist, a researcher in the field of study, or a colleague to verify the application of the methodologies that are incorporated into the lessons.

- Ask a content area specialist to review the lessons to check the sequence in which the methodological skills are taught.

- Check the lessons for balance, variety, sequence, depth of concepts, methodological principles applied, and authentic use of vocabulary from the field of study.

- Field test the activities with students to check for interest. Ask them to rate the activities on a five point scale from dull to exciting. Obtain suggestions from students on what might make the activities or lessons more exciting and interesting.

- Review the lessons to ascertain if graphics, visuals, or technology-supported software and equipment will make the lessons more authentic.

Section IV: Selecting the Representative Topics

Goal Statement:

To select and teach representative topics that apply basic principles, functional concepts, and methodologies in a selected field of study.

Materials Needed:

College Textbooks   Bloom's Taxonomy
Knowledge Menu   Journal Indices and Articles
Instructor Textbook   Research Articles

Steps:

1. Generate a list of topics (facts, trends, conventions, and sequences) that best illustrate the content of the selected field of study. Use the *Representative Topics Template* to list your ideas.

2. Use the following criteria to select the topics to include in your lessons:

   - Do the topics apply, address, or illustrate one of more of the basic principles, functional concepts, or methodological procedures taught earlier in the unit?

   - Will the selected topics interest and motivate the students?

3. Using the Instructional Objectives and Student Activities Menu, the Instructional Strategies Menu, the Instructional Sequence Menu, the Artistic Modification Menu, and the Instructional Products Menu, develop students activities and lessons that will represent the specifics of the field of study. Use the *Multiple Menu Model Unit Plan Template* to storyboard your lesson ideas.

4. Check the validity of your lessons:

   - Do the lessons teach the content and knowledge of a field of study through representative topics that apply basic principles, functional concepts, and methodologies?

   - Check the lessons for balance, variety, depth of concepts and principles applied, and authentic use of vocabulary from the field of study.

   - Field test the activities with content area experts and journal indices to confirm that you have selected representative topics.

- Field test the activities with students to determine interest. Collect suggestions on how to make the lessons more interesting to students.

- Review the lessons to ascertain if graphics, visuals, or technology-supported software and equipment will make the lessons more authentic.

Appendix B

Planning Guide Templates

Knowledge Tree Template

Goal: Design a graphic representation (Knowledge Tree) of a field of study to help students locate and understand the organization of the field of study they will explore. Keep your students in mind as you create the graphic.

Note: You might want to begin with the following categories: Logic, Mathematics, Science, History & Humanities, Philosophy. Add other categories to help you organize and visualize your chosen field of study.

LOGIC   MATHEMATICS   SCIENCE   HISTORY & HUMANITIES   PHILOSOPHY

Gathering Information Template

Goal: To provide the learner with information about where a field is "located" within the broad spectrum of knowledge, the various subdivisions of knowledge within this field, and the specific mission and characteristics of any given subdivision. Use the boxes below to gather information about the field that can be used in planning your introductory lessons.

Purpose	Subdivisions	Questions	Data Sources
Organization	Professional Journals	Available Databases	Chronology of Events
Major Events	Famous People	Places	Predominant Beliefs and Concerns
Best-Case Examples	Trivia, Humor, Meccas	Scandals and Unspoken Beliefs	Abbreviations and Acronyms

Basic Principles, Concepts, and Student Inquiries Template

(Finding the "Big Ideas")

Goal: To select and identify the most important ideas that need to be communicated to the students about the topic. Principles, frequently called the "big ideas" of a field of study, are often stated as relationships among concepts and concisely summarize a great deal of information. Functional concepts are organizers of meaning that are defined and labeled and serve as the working vocabulary of a particular field. After identifying these basic principles and concepts, turn them into inquiries that students can begin to explore.

Field of Study: _____

What are the basic principles which students will explore?	What are the concepts that will need to be developed?	What student inquiries/questions can be developed to assist students in "uncovering" these ideas?

Methodologies Template

Goal: To acquaint students with the methodologies a practicing professional would use to create knowledge.

Field of Study: _____

Professional Occupation: _____

Methodologies:

Representative Topics Template

Goal: To select topics that best illustrate the basic principles and functional concepts.

Field of Study: _____

Basic Principles and Functional Concepts	Representative Topics

Artistic Modification Template

Topic: _____

Direct Experience

Work Related	Travel	Personal Acquaintances	Group Affiliations	Realia / Memorabilia	Personally Significant Event

Indirect (Vicarious) Experience

Fiction	Non-Fiction	Film, Audio, Video Experiences	Fantasy or Simulation

Creative Modification (Output)

Written	Visual	Oral/Performed	Constructed	Leadership Oriented	Film, Video, Computer Program

Multiple Menu Unit Plan Template

Unit Title _____   Section of Knowledge Menu _____   Grade Level _____

Instructional Objectives and Activities

___ Assimilation and Retention

___ Information Analysis

___ Information Synthesis and Application

___ Evaluation

Instructional Strategies

___ Lecture
___ Recitation and Drill
___ Peer Tutoring
___ Discussion
___ Programmed Instruction
___ Role Playing
___ Simulations
___ Replicated Reports or Projects
___ Problem-Based
___ Guided or Unguided Independent Research
___ Other

Storyboarding the Lessons

Instructional Products

Concrete Products
___ Artistic
___ Performance
___ Spoken
___ Visual
___ Models/Constructions
___ Leadership
___ Written

Abstract Products
___ Cognitive Development
___ Affective

Artistic Modification

Student Inquiry Questions

Assessment
___ Product Assessment
___ Interviews/Observations
___ Journals
___ Learning Logs
___ Performance Assessment
___ Oral
___ Multiple Choice
___ Essay
___ Other

Reference Materials/Community Resources

Appendix C

Unit Overviews and Knowledge Trees

Shake, Rattle, and Roll: A Unit on Seismology
by Kari Freidig

The purpose of this unit is to engage students in the process of uncovering the principles, concepts, and methodologies that are involved in the real-world work of geologists. This unit also has direct correlations to the guidelines and content standards of scientific knowledge as established by the State of California for students in grade six.

The unit is based on four principles that represent enduring scientific truths and correlate to the field of geology and seismology. The principles also represent California State standard numbers 1 and 7 as well as many of their subcategories. They are as follows:

1. Earth is in a constant state of change.
2. Plate tectonics produces major geologic events that affect features of the earths surface.
3. Many phenomena on the earth's surface are affected by the transfer of energy.
4. Scientific progress is made by asking meaningful questions and conducting careful investigations.

Fundamental concepts that underlie these principles are used to structure and build the students understanding as they uncover the science that lies within.

Principles	Concepts	Student Inquiries	Methodological Skills
• Earth is in a constant state of change. • Plate tectonics produces major geological events that affect features of the earth's surface. • Many phenomena on the earth's surface are affected by the transfer of energy. • Scientific progress is made by asking meaningful questions and conducting careful investigations.	• Earthquakes • Faults • Epicenter • Energy Transfer • Movement • Seismic Waves • Destruction • Change • Predictions • Force • Cause and Effect • Regeneration • Continent Drift • Plate Tectonics	• What causes earthquakes? • How do geologists know where the epicenter of an earthquake is? • During an earthquake why do some buildings collapse while others remain standing? • What makes a building earthquake resistant? • How do earthquakes cause damage? • How does movement of the plates affect the earth's surface? • What causes movement of the earth's plates? • How do seismic waves travel through the earth? • How do geologists measure earthquakes? • Where do most earthquakes occur? • How do geologists monitor faults? • How do geologists study the earth?	How to • make models. • model movement along faults. • infer how faulting can change the land surface. • classify deformations in surface features caused by different types of faults. • measure, record, and interpret seismic waves. • locate the epicenter of an earthquake. • predict earthquake probability. • use a creep meter to determine the movement of faults. • design, build, and test a model structure that is earthquake resistant. • relate cause and effect to evaluate earthquake damage to a model structure.

TREE OF KNOWLEDGE: SEISMOLOGY

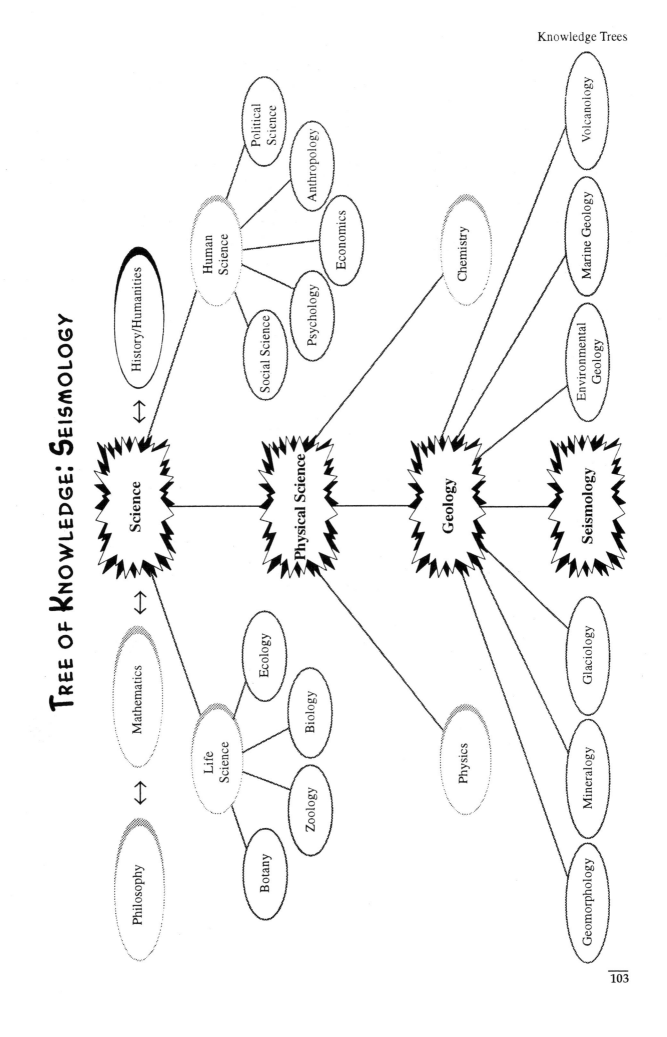

Building Geography: It's More than Maps
by Casey Handfield and Jill Horak

Building Geography: It's More than Maps is an elementary unit of study that can be adapted by teachers of any grade level. Students will be exposed to the materials of this unit through a variety of instructional techniques, but major emphasis will be placed on students uncovering the principles and concepts of the five themes of geography. Acting as the "guides on the side," teachers will facilitate learning activities that will allow students to explore the objectives of individual lessons. The objectives of the lessons in this unit have been constructed so that students become familiar with, and experts on, the five themes of geography.

The specific principles and concepts that students will be introduced to deal with the following:

1. location
2. place
3. region
4. human-environment interactions
5. movement

Understanding location gives students a sense of one's place in time and space and is essential for developing a global perspective. Students will study the concept of location by describing location as relative and absolute.

Place plays a critical role in the success or failure of a civilization. Students will study the principle of place through the concept that the earth has both physical and cultural characteristics that distinguish one area from all other areas. Change in one area is affected by and leads to change in other areas (e.g., an alteration in the physical characteristics of a place can lead to economic, political, or cultural changes). Students will learn about the principle of change by working with the concept that a region is an area with common features that set it apart from other areas.

Living things develop adaptations to their environments that enhance their abilities to survive in those environments or they move to another environment. This principle will be explored through the concept of human-environment interaction. Students will appreciate that all places have advantages and disadvantages for human settlement.

Finally, students will learn that people do not occupy places evenly across the face of the earth. They move from one location to another to interact, trade goods, and communicate with one another.

By giving students a solid foundation in geography, they will gain the working knowledge necessary to compete and cooperate in today's global society. As students uncover the principles of the five themes of geography, they will build a geographer's toolbox that will enable them to extend this unit of study into a personal geographical interest study.

Principles	Concepts	Student Inquiries
A sense of one's place in time and space is essential for the development of a global perspective.	*Location* There are two ways to describe location: relative and absolute.	Where do you live? Where do other people live relative to you? How can you describe location? How does location impact the success of a civilization? What does it mean to live in a desirable location?
Place plays a critical role in the success or failure of a civilization.	*Place* Every place on earth has both physical and cultural characteristics that distinguish it from other places.	What is the geography of your town? What is the geography of the towns near you? How does geography differ throughout the world? Is a culture a result of place or is place a result of the culture?
Change in one area is affected by and leads to change in other areas.	*Region* A region is an area with common features that set it apart from other areas.	What is the geography of your region? What region of the country do you live in? How are other regions similar to or different from yours? Does region influence innovation and change? What geographical features hinder development of a region?
Living things develop adaptations to their environments that enhance their abilities to survive in those environments or they move to other environments.	*Human-Environment Interaction* All places have advantages and disadvantages for human settlement.	What geographical features exist in your town that are helpful or problematic to your town's survival? Are there geographical features that are essential to human survival?
Migration may lead to enhanced opportunities or greater personal freedoms.	*Movement* People do not occupy places evenly across the face of the earth. They move from one location to another to interact, trade goods, and communicate with one another.	What are the most/least populated areas of your town? Why? What are the most/least populated areas of your region? What makes people want to leave their homes?
A cultural geographer seeks to understand the association of human, biological, and physical features on the surface of the earth.	*Methodology* observation, measurement, description, interview, chronology	How can you tell differences between people? What do different areas of the earth look like? Why? What physical features exist on the earth? How do human, biological, and physical features interact?

Knowledge Tree - Building Geography

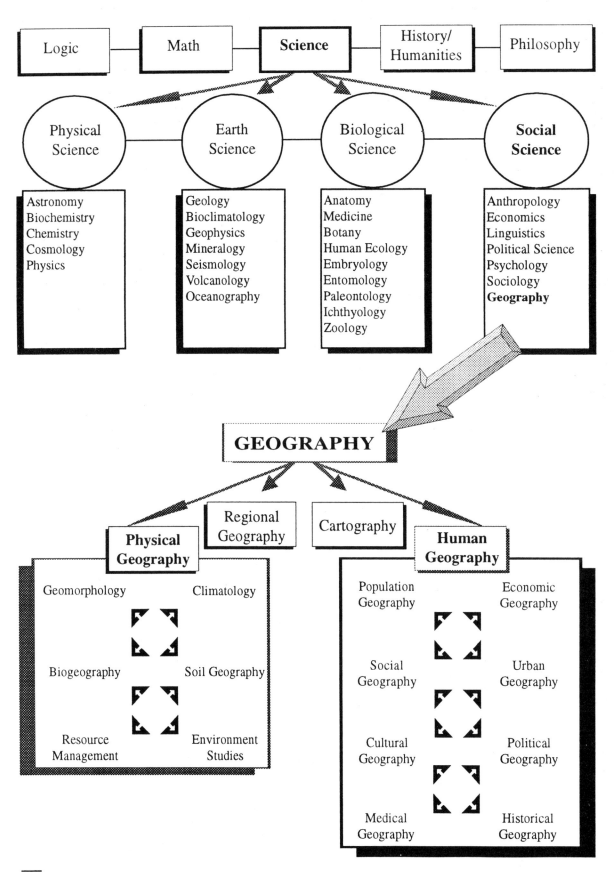

Math Sense: Perceiving Patterns, Making Meaning
A Curriculum for Fourth Grade Mathematics Enrichment
by Olivia Dorfman

"Math Sense" is the mathematician's special mode of perception. Just as the senses of hearing or sight enable our brains to process sound or light waves, "math sense" enables mathematicians to simplify complex phenomena in the world around us. "Math Sense" is also the clear, simple, gut-level understanding of numerical and geometrical relationships, the visceral "making sense" of mathematics that goes beyond rote use of algorithm to a true comprehension of concepts through the hands-on construction of mathematical knowledge. Finally, "Math Sense" is the title for this curriculum unit, which is designed to place students in the roles of mathematicians and thereby experience a deeper process of mathematical learning.

The curriculum is based on four enduring principles:

1. **Mathematics describes order.**

   Mathematics helps human beings find order and structure in their environments. It is a way of describing discoveries about the universe and everything in it.

2. **Mathematics is culturally shaped.**

   Mathematics is a collaborative, intellectual creation shaped by its place in human time and experience (i.e., different cultures invent different mathematics).

3. **Mathematics is ever-changing.**

   Mathematics is a dynamic and continually evolving field of inquiry.

4. **Mathematics is fallible.**

   Mathematics is imperfect and paradoxical and may be inappropriately or incorrectly applied.

Principles	Concepts	Student Inquiries
Mathematics describes order.	abstraction, symbols, algorithms, uses (economics, science, architecture, etc.), classification, deduction, simplicity, rhythm, beauty, patterns	What is math? Why was math created? Why do we need to learn math today? How will we use math as adults?
Mathematics is culturally shaped.	ethnomathematics, technologies, symbols, ancient mathematics (Egyptian, Sumerian)	Who created math? Where did math come from? How has math been different in different parts of the world? How do other forms of mathematics work?
Mathematics is ever-changing.	great mathematicians and their discoveries, computers and calculators	Has the math we use changed over time? Do mathematicians make mistakes? How does mathematics change?
Mathematics is fallible.	paradoxes, unsolved problems, manipulation of statistics, inappropriate application (e.g., in social sciences), fallibility, imperfect structures, implicit bias, a human product that mirrors human nature	Are mathematical answers always right? How does mathematics affect what people believe and what we do? If something is expressed in numbers, why do people think it is more correct? How is data manipulated

The Garden of Knowledge
A Metaphor for the Place of Mathematics in the Grand Scheme of Things

Although one type of relationship between the various disciplines of study can be displayed in a hierarchical tree, other ways in which accumulated knowledge is interrelated might better be illustrated using a visual metaphor. I chose to use an artistic vision, both to symbolize the beauty of mathematics (and all knowledge, for that matter) and to represent the functional connection between mathematics and most other branches of knowledge.

Clearly no discipline is an island, and through time, the cross-pollination of ideas between domains has generated new theories, paradigms, methodologies, and technologies. Now human beings, using computers, continue to develop their capacities for inquiry beyond the scope of the single mind, as increased communication on a global scale has spread the seeds of different cultures' histories, philosophies, and ideas. Just as gardeners through their travels have collected and disseminated the world's plants, sometimes preserving a species on the brink of destruction and sometimes spreading an invasive scourge, the knowledge gardeners of today are tending a vast and beautiful array of disciplines. These gardeners—in my metaphor representing the institutions of education, library science, and information technology—are constantly rearranging the structure of knowledge, creating new patterns of understanding, weeding out some concepts and propagating others. Thus knowledge is presented as an ecological system, tended by humanity, but containing essential truths that are beyond human creation.

The Role of Mathematics in the Garden of Knowledge

The domain of mathematics is represented as a skep, an old fashioned beehive, to suggest bustling activity and a hint of danger. Within the beehive swarm the mathematical bees, normally hidden but partially revealed in my illustration with a cutaway view. The hive at first seems mysterious, even chaotic, but as one acquires more mathematical knowledge, the orderly structure of the bee's society is revealed.

The few bees buzzing about the garden represent the familiar mathematics learned in elementary school—arithmetic, geometry, or simple algebra. The relationship between mathematics and the various disciplines, such as those grouped as the sciences or humanities, is represented by the action of the bees as pollinators essential to the survival of the knowledge growers. Thus the patterns in music or art, the methods used in analyzing research, or the logical structures underlying computer languages are all directly influenced by mathematics. Mathematics, in turn, takes the essences of those flowers and returns with them to the hive where they are turned into fuel for new developments within the field.

Finally, the fact that bees can sting suggests that mathematics is not always benign and can be used for harm in human endeavors. But if people are careful with math, it is delightful, useful, and even entertaining. Listen, and you may hear a buzz—that's mathematics.

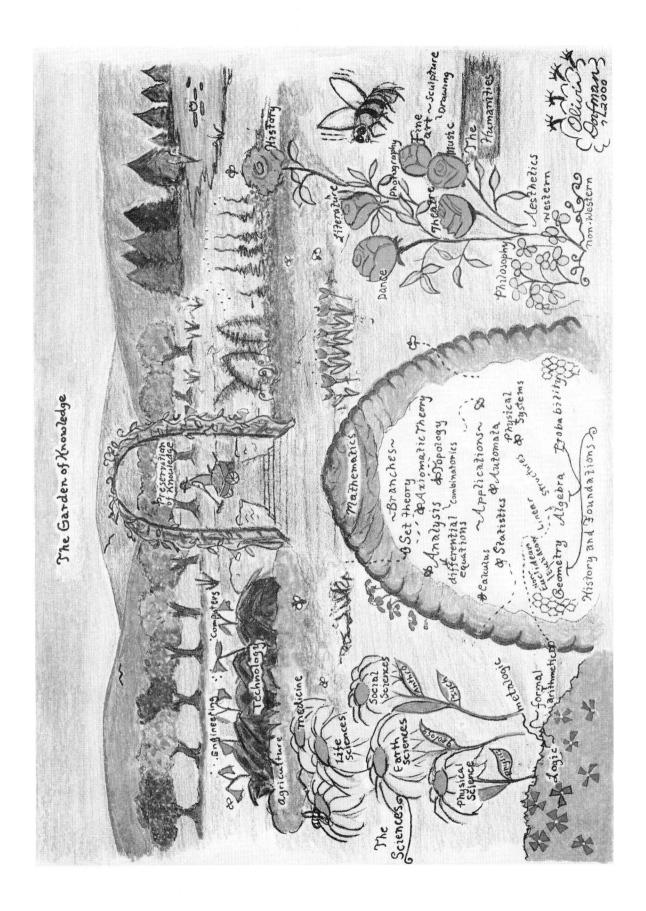

In Search of a Hero
A Problem-Based Curriculum Unit for Grades 5-6
by Deb Young

Rationale and Intent:

The study of individuals and individual identities contributes to our understanding of human behavior. This fundamental principle of the social studies is particularly relevant to the preadolescent child about to enter a developmental stage that often brings emotional upheaval in terms of identity. You may remember that Erik Erickson labeled this emotional upheaval as the "identity crisis." Children of this age are repeatedly trying to define themselves through the question "Who Am I?" as they re-evaluate their self concepts by exploring a variety of social roles.

Professionals in the field of psychology, a discipline which stems from biology, sociology, and anthropology (via the life and social sciences), ask five essential questions as they study the minds and behaviors of individuals:

1. How do human act?
2. How do humans know?
3. How do humans interact?
4. How do human develop?
5. How do human differ from each other?

As students come to understand (through the lens of psychology) *how* the study of individuals and individual identities contributes to our understanding of human behavior, they will be better able to articulate certain psychological constructs that can later be used as tools to facilitate learning in other areas outside this unit. The psychological constructs this unit encompasses include courage, cowardice, altruism, peer pressure, resiliency, adversity, ethics, nature vs. nurture, fight or flight, and the development of character (one's own as well as those encountered in literature and real life). A student who understands the meaning of the concepts of adversity and resiliency, for example, could then connect that understanding to another concept such as the "bootstraps" theory somewhere down the road of his or her learning.

This unit has purposefully been designed around problem-based learning models that demand critical thinking through the stages of creative problem solving. Students will emerge from this unit with their own definition of heroic behavior as well as an understanding of some important concepts from the field of psychology, the discipline of knowledge in which this learning has been situated. To facilitate students' understanding of individual identities, this unit calls upon students to identify literary, historical, and contemporary heroes by identifying and analyzing the character attributes, actions, and behaviors of such individuals. In addition, students will examine their own attributes, actions, and behaviors as they reflect on their own potential to become heroes.

As stated earlier, students will use the methodology of practicing psychologists in conjunction with this unit. They will observe and analyze individual human behaviors as well as form and test hypotheses about why people act the way they do. In addition, this unit integrates content and skills found in student performance objectives from the State of Connecticut language arts frameworks, which requires that students analyze and respond to both fiction and nonfiction and write descriptive, expository, and persuasive text.

In summary, this unit on heroes allows students to reach a cognitive understanding and affective appreciation for differences in human behavior. It is my hope that, upon completion of this unit, students will see more clearly the relevance of studying literature, biographies, and contemporary texts to understand the worth of the individual, both in themselves and in others, and to see how one's attributes, behaviors, and actions contribute to our collective knowledge about human behavior.

Curriculum Overview

This problem-based unit closely models the creative problem solving process of Osborne (1963). As students move through a series of six stages, they will emerge from the "mess" posed in Stage I by reaching acceptance of their solution to the problem in Stage VI.

Stage I: Mess Finding—"Calling All Heroes!"

The unit's objectives are introduced in this phase with the receipt of a copy of an "official" document—a press release to the media that contains an all-call for heroes. This stage has two phases: in the divergent phase of Mess Finding, students will generate a list of potential nominees using the creative thinking methodology of brainstorming. Convergent thinking is necessary in the second phase in order for students to reach a tentative understanding of the construct of hero. Also, they will realize that more information is needed to emerge from the "mess" they have been thrust into.

Stage II: Data Finding—"What is a Hero?"

Students will deepen their understanding of what a hero is as they analyze attributes, behaviors, and deeds of literary, historical, and contemporary heroes. In this second stage of the problem-solving process, teachers should "inject" the terminology of specific psychological constructs such as "fight or flight," "altruism," "resiliency," and "identity" into students' discussions. Using discipline-specific terminology will help students experience the field of psychology in a context that will ensure internalization of these concepts.

Stage III: Problem Finding—"Where Have All the Heroes Gone? The Search for Contemporary Heroes"

In this stage of the problem-solving process, students will ponder the absence or presence of heroes in contemporary society by forming individual hypotheses and conducting "literature reviews" to determine whether they can or cannot find support for their hypotheses. By the end of the stage, using all knowledge gained in the first three stages of the unit, students shall be ready to articulate their cognitive and affective understanding of "hero."

Stage IV: Idea Finding—"My Hero Is . . ."

Here, students will apply the understanding they have constructed in order to determine who they will nominate as their hero. The idea finding stage calls for evaluative thinking through the production of a product (a written analysis) that has a dual purpose: 1) the teacher may use this product to assess student comprehension, and 2) this product is necessary to continue through the subsequent stages in the unit. By nominating their heroes, students will demonstrate conceptual understanding of the construct, "hero."

Stage V: Solution Finding—"A Hero among Heroes"

As the deadline for nominations approaches, students will, in cooperative groups, act as their own selection committees. Who will the class choose as the "Hero among Heroes"? In making this decision, students will generate and reach consensus on the evaluative criteria that will be applied to each student's nomination. In this stage, a solution will be reached—one hero will be nominated for the national monument.

Stage VI: Accepting Finding—"Heroes among Us"

In this final stage of the problem-solving process, students will apply their understanding of character attributes to examine their own hero potentiality. This lesson encompasses all stages of the creative problem-solving model, exercises students' writing skills, and, most importantly, causes students to reflect back upon the essential question upon which this unit is based: how does the study of individuals and individual differences contribute to our understanding of human behavior? Through such reflection, students are forced to become conscious of their own personalities and understand the impact of their own personalities in relation to others.

Osborne, A. F. (1963). *Applied Imagination* (3rd edition). New York: Scribners.

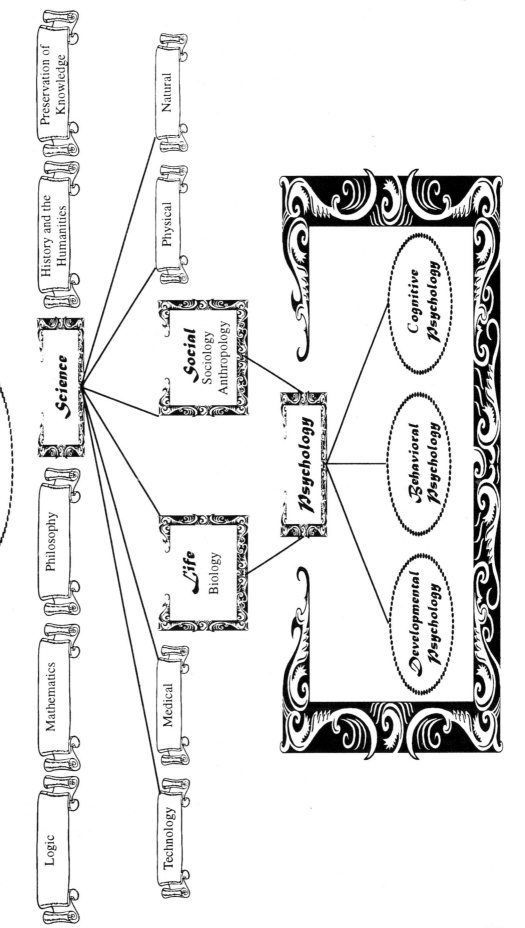

Tree of Knowledge—In Search of a Hero

KNOWLEDGE

Logic
Mathematics
Philosophy
History and the Humanities
Preservation of Knowledge

Science

Technology
Medical

Life
Biology

Social
Sociology
Anthropology

Physical
Natural

Psychology

Developmental Psychology
Behavioral Psychology
Cognitive Psychology

Appendix D

How-to Resources

Aeronautics and Astronomy

Let's Build Airplanes & Rockets! by Drs. Ben P. Millspaugh and Beverley Taylor

Students can build hot air balloons, gliders, or Chuck Yeager's X-1 plane. Each project includes step-by-step instructions, a list of materials, safety guidelines, short biographies of famous aviators, and additional cross-curriculum exercises.
Published by McGraw-Hill. 1996.

Telescope Power by Gregory L. Matloff

Through experiments and activities, aspiring astronomers explore the power of a telescope and learn about different types of telescopes and hardware. Readers take a tour of the universe, hunt for blue lunar flashes, use color filters to observe changing seasons on Mars, visit the Spiral Galaxy in Andromeda, and much more.
Published by John Wiley & Sons. 1993.

Anatomy

Blood and Guts by Linda Allison

Through illustrations, diagrams, and experiments, youngsters can learn how joints work, how acid affects teeth, and how each body part plays an important role in an individual's overall physiology and anatomy.
Published by Little, Brown. 1990.

Archaeology

Hands-On Archaeology: Explore the Mysteries of History through Science by John R. White

With this book, teachers can create simulated archaeological digs in their classrooms or on field trips in their communities. Students learn the same methods as practicing archaeologists: how to grid, design, and organize a site; classify, handle, and preserve artifacts; and more.
Published by Prufrock Press. 1998.

Architecture and Design

The Art of Construction: Projects and Principles for Beginning Engineers & Architects by Mario Salvadori

Using historical examples from caves to skyscrapers, this resource takes students through the principles of engineering and architecture. Project suggestions using household items give students a hands-on understanding of all aspects of structure and design.
Published by Chicago Review Press. 1990.

KidTech: Hands-On Problem Solving with Design Technology by Lucy Miller

Sixty activities integrate design technology and real-world problems into the curriculum. Students use their creativity and critical thinking skills to design and build toys, gadgets, moving ads, and more. Also included are tips for setting up classrooms; basic techniques for construction, movement, and power; and assessment resources.
Published by Dale Seymour Publications. 1998.

Why Design? Activities and Projects from the National Building Museum by Anna Slafer and Kevin Cahill

A myriad of projects and activities help learners explore what constitutes good design. Students discover how a designer progresses from a problem to a creative solution, how

cultural values shape an environment, how to develop and edit ideas, how to select the right building material, and how to present ideas.
Published by Chicago Review Press. 1995.

Art

Conversations in Paint by Charles Dunn

This comprehensive introduction to the fundamentals of painting offers readers part painter's sketchbook, part philosopher's journal, and part instructor's primer. Illustrations and engaging text present both elemental information to novices and new ways of approaching painting to experienced artists.
Published by Workman Publishing. 1996.

Discovering Great Artists: Hands-On Art for Children in the Styles of the Great Masters by MaryAnn F. Kohl and Kim Solga

Short biographies of famous artists such as Lorenzo Ghiberti, Mary Cassatt, Salvadore Dali, and Carl Van Allsburg along with intriguing activities encourage youngsters to learn about the contributions these artists have made while exploring the artist's particular style.
Published by Bright Ideas Press. 1996.

The Great T-Shirt Book! by Carol Taylor

Youngsters interested in fashion design can expand their wardrobes using a variety of techniques including batik, tie-dye, marbling, block printing, and screen printing.
Published by Lark Books. 1992.

An Introduction to Acrylics by Ray Smith (1998)
An Introduction to Drawing by James Horton (1998)
An Introduction to Mixed Media by Michael Wright (1999)
An Introduction to Perspective by Ray Smith (1999)
An Introduction to Watercolor by Ray Smith (1998)

Whether readers have taken art classes or never held a drawing pen or artist's brush, the titles in this series present everything students need to know about working in a variety of mediums. Easy-to-follow projects, illustrated in steps, teach the essentials while inspiring students to tackle more difficult techniques.
Published by DK Publishing.

Handmade Books and Cards by Jean G. Kropper

Detailed instructions, full-color photographs, and line drawings guide aspiring bookmakers as they learn binding techniques (from basic pamphlet binding to concertina binding) and how to make hard covers. Also included are inspiring ideas for alternative book formats, greeting cards, and even sculptures.
Published by Davis Publications. 1997.

Origami Inspired by Japanese Prints by Steve and Megumi Biddle

Because origami is an ancient Japanese art form, it naturally follows that reproductions of color woodprints by Japanese masters be the inspiration for origami projects. Step-by-step instructions show learners how to make origami birds, flowers, insects, animals, and even a kimono! Text written by a curator of Japanese art from the Metropolitan Museum of Art explains the significance of each artifact.
Published by Viking Childrens Books. 1998.

Business and Investing

Better than a Lemonade Stand: Small Business Ideas for Kids by Daryl Bernstein

Along with specific business ideas ranging from cleaning things to profiting from a special talent, fifteen-year-old Daryl Bernstein introduces the general information and skills necessary for running a successful business. Tips on keeping consumers happy, setting a selling price, and handling loans are all included.
Published by Beyond Words Publishing. 1992.

Growing Money by Gail Karlitz

A complete investing guide for kids, *Growing Money* explains the difference between stocks and bonds, how to read the financial pages, the lowdown on savings banks, the buying and selling of stocks, and more.
Published by Price Stern Sloan Publishing. 1999.

Playing the Market by Karen Isaacson

Just like investors around the world do everyday, students learn how to choose stocks, report and calculate commissions, and track the value of their investments.
Published by Dale Seymour Publications. 2000.

Calligraphy

Calligraphy by Caroline Young

This book clearly illustrates techniques and equipment for 15 calligraphy styles as well as stenciling, rubbing, embossing, and incising. Suggestions for real-world projects include designing a new alphabet and making cards, name plates, and presents.
Published by EDC Publishing. 1990.

Creative Calligraphy by Pete Halliday

Creative Calligraphy explains how to draw decorative lettering without special pens and equipment. Readers learn about different lettering styles and how they can be used, design monograms and word pictures, and use decorative lettering to make invitations, cards, posters, books, and mobiles.
Published by Larousee Kingfisher Chambers. 2000.

Cartooning

The Complete Book of Caricature by Bob Staake

Short biographies of great caricaturists such as Al Hirschfield, David Levine, Michael White along with hundreds of examples offer readers a chance to receive mentoring from the masters. Topics covered include the role or roles of caricature, how to develop style, how to capture personality in facial features, and different venues for caricatures.
Published by North Light Books. 1991.

The Creative Cartoonist: A Step-by-Step Guide for the Aspiring Amateur by Dick Gautier

Illustrations and step-by-step instructions show aspiring cartoonists how to draw the human face and figure. All the fundamentals of cartooning are included: materials, basic techniques, and a host of crazy characters to draw.
Published by Perigee. 1989.

Creative Writing and Publishing

The Art and Craft of Playwriting by Jeffrey Hatchen

Using examples from successful plays such as *Six Degrees of Separation* and *Hedda Gabler*, Hatchen illustrates the elements of a great play. Writing exercises help students practice techniques such as creating tension and conflict, linking the point of attack and the climax, and developing play ideas. Interviews with playwrights offer insight into the mindset and technique of writing plays.
Published by Story Press. 1996.

Creating a Page-Turner by Janice Jones

This helpful guide shows students in grades 3-8 how to write good fiction and includes suggestions for selecting a setting, creating exciting characters, organizing an interesting plot, using descriptive language, grabbing the reader's attention, inventing catchy titles, and revising story elements and grammar.
Published by Creative Learning Press, Inc. 1995.

The Creative Writing Handbook by Jay Amberg and Mark Larson

Each self-contained unit in this resource provides the framework and materials needed to build skills in writing narratives, short fiction, and poetry. Also included are prewriting activities, clear drafting directions, editing and proofing activities, and more.
Published by Scott Foresman. 1992.

Painting the Sky: Writing Poetry with Children by Shelley Tucker

Shelley Tucker demystifies poetry and helps young students learn how to write with metaphors, similes, personification, and other poetic elements. Exercises and activities help students learn new ways of expressing themselves and the things they see.
Published by Goodyear Publishing. 1995.

A Teen's Guide to Getting Published by Danielle Dunn and Jessica Dunn

Written by teens for teens, this guide covers every aspect of getting published from editing and revising work to requesting manuscript guidelines and working with editors. A directory of publications and contests and additional resources for young writers are also included.
Published by Prufrock Pres. 1997.

Writing Poetry by Shelley Tucker

Tucker defines 14 poetic elements in easy-to- understand terms with both the beginner and experienced poet in mind. Examples of poems written by people of all ages illustrate each element, and exercises and writing ideas give readers a chance to practice techniques.
Published by Scott Foresman. 1992.

The Young Person's Guide to Becoming a Writer by Janet E. Grant

This practical, inspiring guide to starting and maintaining a writing career helps young writers experiment with different genres, evaluate their own work, locate publishers, prepare and submit work, and more. Also included are suggestions and success stories from other young writers and a list of books for further reading.
Published by Free Spirit Publishing. 1995.

Entomology

Monarch Magic! by Lynn M. Rosenblatt

From a tiny egg to caterpillar to beautiful monarch, youngsters can follow the life and migratory patterns of monarch butterflies through compelling text and full-color photo-

graphs. Throughout are engaging activities, journal ideas, crafts, and more.
Published by Willliamson Publishing. 1998.

Pet Bugs: A Kid's Guide to Catching & Keeping Touchable Insects by Sally Kneidel (1994)
More Pet Bugs by Sally Kneidel (1999)

Each chapter in *Pet Bugs* introduces a particular insect (or insect relative) and presents
information on how and where to find it, how to catch it and keep it in captivity, and
interesting aspects of the insect's behavior. *More Pet Bugs* includes small creatures such
as earthworms, slugs and snails, and other creatures.
Published by John Wiley & Sons.

Genealogy

How to Tape Instant Oral Biographies by William Zimmerman

Newly revised, this resource shows youngsters how to create a library filled with spoken
histories from various family members and friends. It includes forms for recording family
names, dates, and other data and explains audio and videotape techniques and interviewing and questioning strategies.
Published by Betterway Publications. 1999.

Genealogy Online: Researching Your Roots by Elizabeth Powell Crowe

With the explosion of the Internet and the World Wide Web, genealogical information has
never been more accessible. This resource presents genealogists of all levels with tips for
searching for information on ancestors from around the world, looking through on-line card
catalogues, placing queries on The National Genealogical Society's bulletin board, and more.
Published by McGraw-Hill. 1998.

Unpuzzling Your Past: A Basic Guide to Genealogy, 3rd. Edition by Emily Anne Croom

Croom presents all the tools family detectives need to research their past, including
interview formats, sample letters, worksheets, and addresses. She also includes a
comprehensive resource section, information on deciphering old-fashioned script, tips for
finding out personality traits and physical features of distant relatives, and more.
Published by Betterway Publications. 1995.

Writing Family Histories and Memoirs by Kirk Polking

Kirk Polking helps genealogists first locate family history information and then turn dates
and names into engaging stories. Chapter topics include locating information from
courthouse records, interviewing techniques, making genealogical charts, handling legal
issues, and knowing how much research is enough. Samples of written histories and tips
on good writing techniques are included.
Published by Writer's Digest Books. 1995.

General Science

Fun with Your Microscope by Shar Levine and Leslie Johnstone

Great photographs, drawings, and winning science fair suggestions inspire young
scientists to discover and examine ordinary objects. Students learn about the different
parts of a microscope, various slide preparation techniques, and the importance of
keeping a journal to record findings.
Published by Sterling Publishing. 1999.

Science Fair Survival Techniques for Kids, Parents, and Teachers by the Wild Goose
Company

Young scientists learn how to ask the right questions to develop science fair projects.

Orienteering activities introduce students to a particular topic, and each activity is followed by some possible science projects based on the topic just explored. The "On Your Own" section offers more challenging experiments and extension suggestions. *Published by The Wild Goose Company. 1997.*

Science Without Answers by B.K. Hixson

Children can solve these challenging scientific puzzles by themselves or with friends. Young learners explore the scientific method and develop cooperative learning skills by conducting 25 experiments that investigate topics such as chemistry, botany, electricity, energy, flight, air pressure, biology, optical illusions, and physics. *Published by Wild Goose. 1989.*

Geography

The Book of Where, or How to Be Naturally Geographic by Neill Bell

Students start their journey into geography at home by making maps of their bedrooms. Each successive chapter expands the world from bedrooms to towns, states, the nation, and finally the whole world. Interesting stories about regions in the U.S., activities on map reading, and quizzes about time zones all make geography fun and engaging. *Published by Little, Brown. 1982.*

Geography Wizardry for Kids by Phyllis S. Williams and Margaret Kinda

Over 150 fun projects, maps, games, crafts, and experiments, explore earth, ocean, weather, and animal mysteries. Geography becomes more than places to memorize, it becomes an opportunity to explore the world. *Published by Barrons. 1997.*

History

The Story in History by Margot Fortunato Galt

Students can learn about American history by reexperiencing it as an imaginative writer. Using sources such as early maps, Walt Whitman's account of the Civil War, Sioux Indian oral histories, diaries from women on the Oregon Trail, and their own historical research, learners explore events as professional historians do. Their research culminates in their own historical accounts. *Published by Teachers & Writers Collaborative. 1992.*

Inventing

Inventing Stuff by Ed Sobey

Students learn to invent in terms of solving problems. Sections include information on keeping a journal, inventing backwards, and finding new uses for things as well as facts about inventors and inventions. Information about invention contests help youngsters find outlets for their inventions. *Published by Dale Seymour Publishing 1995.*

Leadership

160 Ways to Help the World: Community Service Projects for Young People by Linda Leeb Duper

Young leaders learn how to develop and implement service projects such as starting a toy collection, sewing blankets for shelters, and sponsoring safety awareness campaigns. Along with step-by-step instructions, the author includes tips on obtaining support from businesses, handling money, and generating publicity. A resource list of community

service publications and organizations is also included.
Published by Checkmark Books. 1996.

The Kid's Guide to Social Action: How to Solve the Social Problems You Choose and Turn Creative Thinking into Positive Action by Barbara Lewis

Along with a collection of stories about real kids who are making a difference, Barbara Lewis explains and gives examples of social action power skills such as letter writing, interviewing, speech-making, fund raising, and arranging media coverage. Samples of actual projects and blank forms help interested students turn their creative thinking into positive action.
Published by Free Spirit Publishing. 1998.

Mathematics

A Blueprint for Geometry by Brad Fulton and Bill Lombard

This resource presents a 2-3 week project in which students become junior architects. Using the blueprints provided, learners make scale drawings, compute building costs, correct elevations, plan the number of electrical outlets and light switches for a room, and answer other questions architects and contractors deal with every day.
Published by Dale Seymour Publishing. 1998.

Mathematical Investigations: A Series of Situational Lessons, Book One by Randall Sonvinery

Covering topics in geometry, patterns, operations research, photography, and genetics, students learn to approach real-world math with creativity and flexibility. Each problem guides students through operations, helping them make their own conjectures, verify assertions, and explain their reasoning. Extension activities present a chance to practice skills or delve into an interesting topic.
Published by Dale Seymour Publishing. 1990.

Math for Smarty Pants by Marilyn Burns

Even math-haters will enjoy this cartoon-packed book that covers arithmetic, geometry, logic, statistics, and games. Youngsters can make and play math games, create a wobbly cube, solve the calendar caper, or become a pollster. Entertaining stories, fascinating facts, and intriguing activities make math an engaging subject for everyone.
Published by Little, Brown. 1982.

Real Life Math Mysteries by Mary Ford Washington

An assistant city engineer poses a problem with runoff water drainage; an architectural estimator needs to determine the cost of constructing a building; a fire fighter must figure how fast to pump water on a fire to extinguish it. Students learn real-world application of important math skills while also learning about a variety of careers.
Published by Prufrock Press. 1995.

Music

Musical Instruments by Meryl Doney

Using everyday objects and easy-to-follow instructions, young musicians can make instruments from around the world. Projects also include information on why and where each instrument evolved.
Published by Franklin Watts. 1995.

Rubber-Band Banjos and a Java Jive Bass by Alex Sabbeth

Students explore how sounds are made and how humans hear them, find out how instruments create music, and learn how to make their own musical instruments. Step-by-step instructions and illustrations guide readers through dozens of projects and experiments involving music and sound.
Published by John Wiley & Sons. 1997.

Paleontology

Make-a-Saurus: My Life with Raptors and Other Dinosaurs by Brian Cooley and Mary Ann Wilson

Readers follow artist Brian Cooley as he creates dinosaur sculptures for museums around the world. He explains how he came to his profession and the research he does on each dinosaur project as he produces dinosaur sculptures for display. He then offers youngsters the opportunity to make their own dinosaurs following the same or similar techniques that he uses.
Published by Annick Press. 2000.

Photography and Videography

How to Make Your Own Video by Perry Schwartz

Perry Schwartz explains the elements of storytelling and the technical basics needed to make a great video. Students learn about what to look for (and avoid) in a camcorder, how to prepare a video shoot, how to write a video script, concepts such as depth of field and composition, and camera angles, shots, and special effects.
Published by First Avenue. 1991.

KidVid: Fun-Damentals of Video Production by Kaye Black

Clear illustrations and text introduce students to the basic equipment and techniques of video production. Nine easy lessons take the reader through scripts, story boards, program treatment, production, editing, and evaluation.
Published by Zephyr Press. 2000.

Photography by Andrew Haslam

Students learn to create their own simple pinhole cameras as well as a tripod and a camera which uses 35mm film. In addition, kids discover how to light a shot and how to process, develop, and print film, make enlargements, and create short movies.
Published by Two-Can Publishing. 1996.

Usborne Guide to Photography by Moira Butterfield and Susan Peach

Clear step-by-step instructions offer advice on all aspects of photography, from operating a camera to developing film. Tips focus on the best way to take pictures, special effects, and how to avoid common mistakes.
Published by EDC Publishing. 1991.

Public Speaking

How to Debate by Robert E. Dunbar

This nuts and bolts guide presents information on types of debates, how to prepare, methods of arguments, effective delivery, listening and responding to the opponent, and how debates are judged. Examples of successful arguments from speakers such as President Lincoln, William F. Buckley, Jr., and Edmund Burke are also included.
Published by Franklin Watts. 1994.

The Public Speaking Handbook by Susan J. Benjamin

In addition to tips on gathering and organizing information and writing a persuasive speech, Susan Benjamin offers instruction on how to effectively use nonverbal communication, maintain audience interest, use the voice to express meaning, and much more. *Published by Good Year Publishing. 1996.*

Research

Looking For Data in All the Right Places by Alane J. Starko and Gina D. Schack (1992)
Research Comes Alive! by Gina D. Schack and Alane J. Starko (1998.

Teachers can use *Looking for Data in All the Right Places* to help elementary-grade students learn how to gather and analyze data in order to answer their research questions. Each chapter includes explanations, examples, and practice activities for different steps of the research process. *Research Comes Alive!* covers many of the same topics, but provides more depth for middle- and high-school students.
Published by Creative Learning Press, Inc.

A Student's Guide to Conducting Social Science Research by Barbara Bunker, Howard Pearlson, and Justin Schultz

This guide discusses the relationship between research and real-life experiences and provides a nine-step approach to research. Students gain experience with data gathering techniques through hands-on activities, and chapters present information about research design, surveys, observations, experiments, and more.
Published by Creative Learning Press, Inc. 1999.

Take Ten...Steps to Successful Research by Liz Rothlein and Anita Meyer Meinbach

By breaking research into ten logical and enjoyable steps, the authors of this resource teach students lifelong skills in analysis, evaluation, and synthesis. Each chapter focuses on one of ten steps such as choosing the subject, selecting appropriate reference materials, writing an outline, and writing the final copy.
Published by Scott Foresman. 1991.

Theater

Acting and Directing by Russell J. Grandstaff

This introduction to acting and directing discusses how these two key elements work together to create professional productions. The acting section covers expressive use of voice and body, building and refining characterizations, stage orientation and use, and performing. The directing section focuses on both prerehearsal and rehearsal responsibilities of the director.
Published by Passport Books. 1990.

Acting and Theatre by Cheryl Evans and Lucy Smith

Readers learn about some of the ways actors train and rehearse, as well as the practical arts of set, prop, and costume design and the technical basics of lighting and sound.
Published by EDC Publishing. 1992.

The Most Excellent Book of How to Be a Puppeteer by Roger Lade

This complete resource contains instructions for making different types of puppets, hints and tips for operating them, and ideas for making theaters.
Published by Copper Beech Books. 1996.

References

References

Ausubel, D. P. (1968). *Educational psychology: A cognitive view.* New York: Holt, Rinehart and Winston.

Ausubel, D. P., Novak, J. D., & Hanesian, H. (1978). *Educational psychology: A cognitive view* (2nd ed.). New York: Holt, Rinehart, and Winston.

Bandura, A. (1977). Self-efficacy: Toward a unifying theory of behavioral change. *Psychological Review, 84,* 191-215.

Bloom, B. S. (Ed.) (1954). *Taxonomy of educational objectives. Handbook I: Cognitive domain.* New York: Longman.

Brandwein, P. (1987). On avenues to kindling wide interests in elementary school: Knowledges and values. *Roeper Review, 10* (1), 32-40.

Bruner, J. S. (1960). *The process of education.* Cambridge, MA: Harvard University Press.

Bruner, J. S. (1966). *Toward a theory of instruction.* Cambridge, MA: Harvard University Press.

Dewey, J. (1916). *Democracy and education: An introduction to the philosophy of education.* New York: The Free Press.

Follett, K. (1995). *A place called freedom.* New York: Crown Publishers.

Gagné, R. M., & Briggs, L. J. (1979). *Principles of instructional design* (2nd ed.). New York: Holt, Rinehart and Winston.

Glickman, C. (1991). Pretending not to know what we know. *Educational Leadership, 48* (8), 4-10.

Goodlad, J. I. (1984). *A place called school: Prospects for the future.* New York: McGraw-Hill.

Hume, I. N. (1996). *In search of this and that: Tales from an archaeologist's quest.* Williamsburg: VA: The Colonial Williamsburg Foundation.

James, W. (1885). On the functions of cognition. *Mind, 10,* 27-44.

Kaplan, S. N. (1986). The grid: A model to construct differentiated curriculum for the gifted. In Renzulli, J. S. (Ed.). *Systems and models for developing programs for the gifted and talented.* Mansfield Center, CT: Creative Learning Press.

National Council for the Social Studies. (1994). *Expectations of Excellence: Curriculum Standards for Social Studies.* Waldorf, Maryland: NCSS Publications.

Nickerson, R. S. (1981). Thoughts about teaching thinking. *Educational Leadership, 39* (1), 21-24.

Nixon, H. L. (1976). *Sport and social organization.* Indianapolis: Bobbs Merrill Co.

Passow, A. H. (1982). *Differentiated curricula for the gifted/talented.* Venture, CA: Leadership Training Institute on the Gifted and Talented.

Phenix, P. H. (1964). *Realms of meaning.* New York: McGraw-Hill.

Phenix, P. H. (1987). *Views on the use, misuse, and abuse of instructional materials.* Paper presented at the Annual Meeting of the Leadership Training Institute on the Gifted and Talented, Houston, TX.

Renzulli, J. S. (1977). *The enrichment triad model: A guide for developing defensible programs for the gifted.* Mansfield Center, CT: Creative Learning Press.

Renzulli, J. S. (1982). What makes a problem real? Stalking the illusive meaning of qualitative differences in gifted education. *Gifted Child Quarterly, 26* (4), 49-59.

Scholastic, Inc. (1996). *Meet the mentor video, Dr. Ruben Mendoza, Archaeologist: Managing information series.* New York: Scholastic, Inc.

Tomlinson, C. A. (1999). *The differentiated classroom: Responding to the needs of all learners.* Alexandria, VA: Association for Supervision and Curriculum Development.

Ward, V. S. (1960). Systematic intensification and extensification of the school curriculum. *Exceptional Children, 28,* 67-71,77.

Ward, V. S. (1961). *Educating the gifted: An axiomatic approach.* Columbus: Merrill.

Whitehead, A. N. (1929). The rhythm of education. In Whitehead, A. N. (Ed.) *The aims of education.* New York: Macmillan.

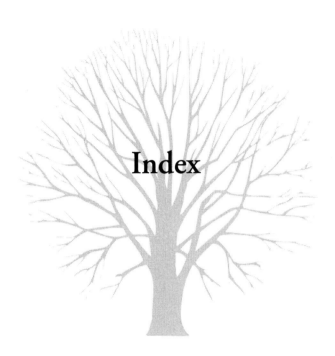

Index

Index

P

R

S

T

U

W